information contained within this document, including, but not limited to, errors, omissions, or inaccuracies.

Table of Contents

Book 1: Needle Felting for Beginners

BEGINNER + INTERMEDIATE GUIDE TO NEEDLE FELTING

ARI YOSHINOBU

CONCLUSION 101

REFERENCES.. 106

Book 2: Intermediate Guide to Needle Felting

TIME TO GET READY...1

CHAPTER 1: 5

NEEDLE FELTING TIPS AND TRICKS....................5

CHAPTER 2: 17

WANDERING WOLF...17

NEEDLE FELTING
FOR
BEGINNERS

ARI YOSHINOBU

Introduction

Crafting is a great way to keep yourself busy and be productive in your downtime. You can also make homemade gifts if you are good at a craft. But it can be hard to find a craft that interests you, is not too hard to learn, and does not require a lot of supplies to get started. Making a major investment to learn a craft is a lot to ask if you do not even know that you will be good at it or enjoy it!

Luckily, needle felting is a craft that is easy to learn and does not require a lot of supplies. This book will give you an overview of the supplies that you need to get started, as well as what you might want to invest in to step up your game after you learn the process.

There are also step-by-step instructions that will help you learn the basics. You will get a chance to try your hand at several different designs, starting with flat designs and progressing to three-dimensional (3D) sculptures.

Once you understand the basic process, you will have no problem creating your own projects. Wait until you see how easy needle felting can be, and how cute the final products look! You will love making these items for yourself, your family and others.

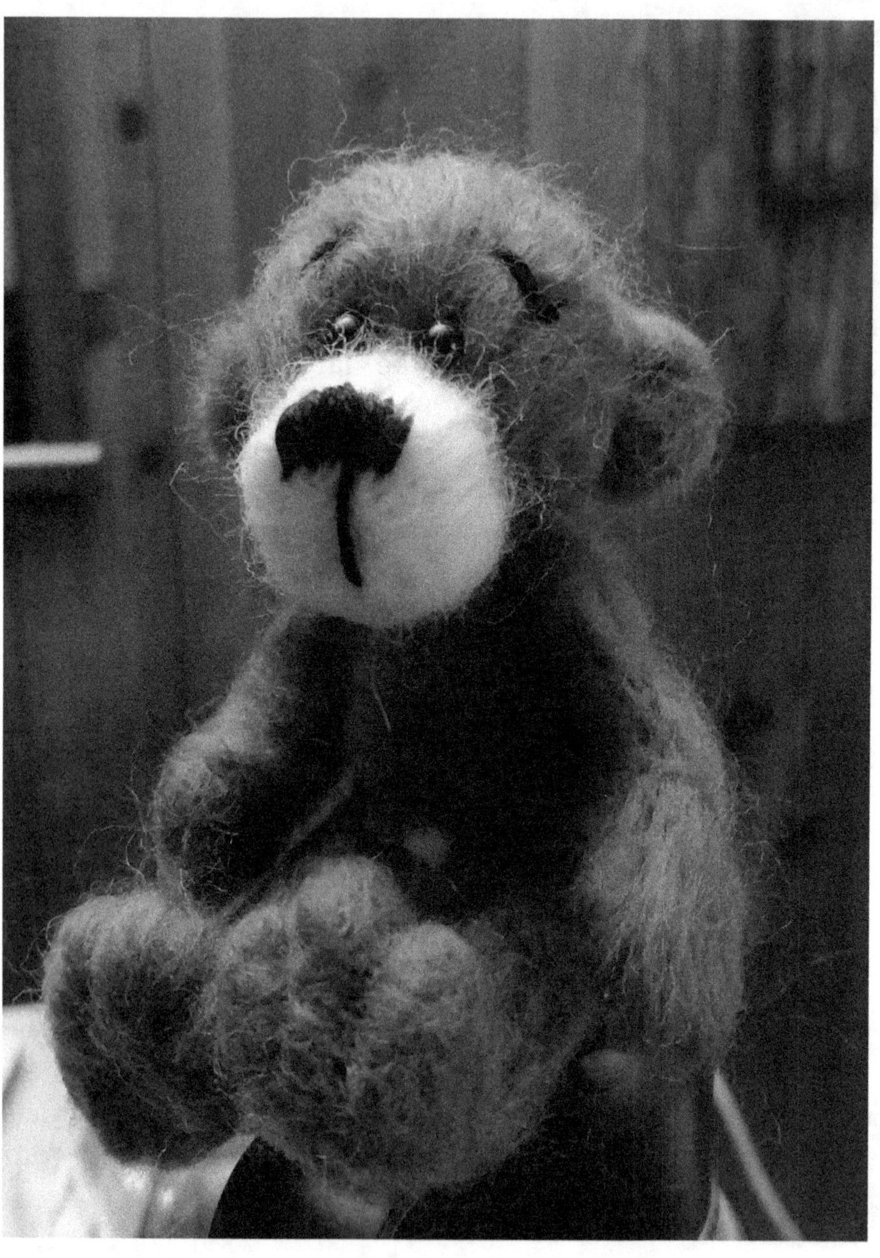

Chapter 1:

Needle Felting

Felting is a way to make wool or cotton into a piece of fabric by connecting the individual fibers. This is one of the few ways of creating fabric that does not involve weaving or spinning. Felting changes the texture of the wool and allows you to do more with it than you could with just the loose fibers. There are many ways of felting, including knitting a project and then felting, wet felting, dry felting, and needle felting.

Needle felting might sound like a very involved process that involves various machines, but it is a project that you can do easily by hand. Needle felting allows you to create 3D objects from a piece of cotton or wool. Using a barbed needle, you work the fibers of the fabric so that they bond together and feel solid. This is a very hands-on craft that enables you to transform loose fiber into a picture that you have in your mind.

After you make the cute designs from this book, you will understand how the texture can be worked into shapes, and you will be able to create your own ideas from scratch. The basic techniques of needle felting are easy to learn and, as you work through the provided patterns, you will start to create your own patterns.

What is Needle Felting?

Basically, needle felting is a method by which to compress loose fibers into a single fabric. This means that you are tangling fibers into a matted piece somewhat like the matted fur sometimes found on long haired pets or the proverbial rat's nest of tangled hair, only needle felting is cleaner and way more fun!

As you start matting a piece of fabric, you can decide what you want to create from it. Since all felting starts as agitating fibers into a tangle, you can start working while you let your imagination run wild. You can keep your project on a flat surface as you needle felt and make flat designs. Just because your felting project is flat does not mean it has to be a square or rectangle sheet! Using cookie cutters and stencils, you can make flat felt projects of different shapes.

You can then take those flat fabrics and shape them into different 3D sculptures. While you are felting, you can also easily shape the fibers to make them look like certain characters or objects. Needle felting sculptures of animals is really popular, and you will learn to make plenty of them in this book.

A perk of needle felting is that you can also use this method to mend clothes! You can use flat felted fabrics as patches on clothes. Once you understand how needle felting works, you might even feel confident enough to use this skill to repair your sweaters and socks!

A Brief History of Needle Felting

In the mid-1970s, Eleanor Stanwood learned to shear the sheep that she was raising in Vermont. By the 1980s, wool was a less popular textile since cotton is much more versatile. Cotton is cheaper to buy, can be made into anything, and is machine washable. In the interest of not wasting wool, Stanwood started turning the fibers into batting before wet felting the material to add layers to bed comforters. After experimenting with a needle punching machine, Stanwood found that she could make scarves, and even sturdier 3D designs. She started using this technique to make jewelry. Stanwood sings the praises of needle felting because the jewelry it makes is biodegradable and can be composted.

Other fiber artists learned this technique and needle felting grew in popularity. To name a few:

Ayala Talpai, inspired by Stanwood, wrote the first book on needle felting: *The felting needle—From factory to fantasy.* Talpai has also written a needle felting workbook and leads workshops in the community and in public schools. Talpai has supported herself as an artist by selling her needle felting crafts at local markets and making wedding garments.

Kay Petal makes needle felted dolls of famous people, and many celebrities have commissioned her work! Petal won her first award for a needle felted Albert Einstein doll less than a year after she started practicing. She said, "I never knew I was artistic until I started needle felting," which should inspire you to try this craft regardless of your previous experience—or lack thereof!

Sara Renzulli is known for her posable needle felted animal sculptures, and teaches workshops on the craft. Her website,

Sarafina Fiber Art, includes access to tutorials, videos for beginners, and online workshops.

Other Types of Felting

Needle felting is a great hands-on craft, but while you are learning about needle felting, you might want to know a brief overview of other kinds of felting as well. The goal of all the different types of felting is to turn loose wool fibers, also called roving, into a cohesive fabric. This fabric can be flat, and used to make other garments or works of arts. This fabric can also be 3D, and shaped into sculptures, statues, and stuffed animals.

Wet Felting

Wet felting is a process that uses water, soap, wool, friction, and pressure to turn loose wool fibers into felt fabric. The soap and water act together to open up the fibers so that they easily catch onto each other. The movement of your hands or a textured surface against the soapy wet wool creates friction, which helps to push the fibers together and makes them become matted and tangled. Like needle felting, wet felting can be used to create flat or three-dimensional objects.

Wet felting can make thick sheets of fabric that can be sewn together into complete garments. This is a nice way to make wool clothing without having to learn to knit or crochet! You will get the heft, warmth, and look of wool without having to weave the yarn fibers together.

You do not have to make sheets of fabric with the wool felting process. Other ways of wool felting create fabrics that look completely different than how you usually picture wool!

Cobweb Felting

Cobweb felting is a method that makes a lightweight felted fabric with a 'cobwebby' texture. Instead of making a thick sheet of felted wool, cobweb felting makes a light and airy fabric with more thin than thick areas. There might even be stylish holes in places!

Instead of using a needle to tangle the roving together, you start cobweb felting by gently pulling the roving apart. The fibers will just barely stay attached to each other, but you will be pulling fibers apart to make thin areas and gaps. You will thin the wool roving until it is about twenty-five percent longer and twenty-five percent wider than you want your scarf to be. Wet felting will cause the fibers to shrink.

After you get the wool roving pulled thin, completely wet it with a spray bottle that has a few drops of soap added, and then start to agitate the fibers with your hands. You can also roll the fabric up in bubble wrap or another bumpy, flexible surface. After a lot of agitation, you can give your fabric a pinch test. You pinch it between your thumb and first finger, and pull up. If the fibers stay together, you have felted it enough. If the roving pulls apart, then you need to add a bit of water and keep working the fibers.

When you unroll your fiber, you wad it up and drop it on the table over and over again. This helps the fibers to adhere to each other so that they start to become a fabric. At this point, you will notice that the fibers have shrunk and puckered. After you wash out the soap and let it dry, you will have a cobweb felted piece of fabric.

Lattice Felting

Lattice felting is a wet wool felting technique which produces a fabric that has holes deliberately added into it. This is because to make the fabric, you will lay out the wool roving in a lattice pattern, almost like a loose weave, and felt the wool with the holes in place.

Like with cobweb felting, you will need to thin your wool roving out before you make a lattice design. Thinner wool actually makes the felting process easier because it will get completely wet which makes it easier to agitate the fibers.

First you lay out the thin pieces of wool roving all in one direction. Then you take more thin strips of wool roving and put them on top of the first layer but in the opposite direction. This creates the lattice pattern that looks like weaving. You can keep the design straight or you can make it look more haphazard and artsy.

Spray the wool roving generously with a spray bottle of water that has a few drops of soap added. Create friction on the fibers by working them with your hands. You can also use bubble wrap or a bumpy surface, just as you did for the cobweb felting. After felting the fibers a bit, wet them again so that they are completely saturated.

You will repeatedly drop your fabric just as you would for cobweb felting. Remember, this process makes the fibers shrink and harden and that completes the felting process. Do the pinch test once again, making sure that the fibers stay together when you try to pull them up. Rinse the soap out, let the piece dry, and enjoy your unique lattice felt fabric.

Felt Fabric

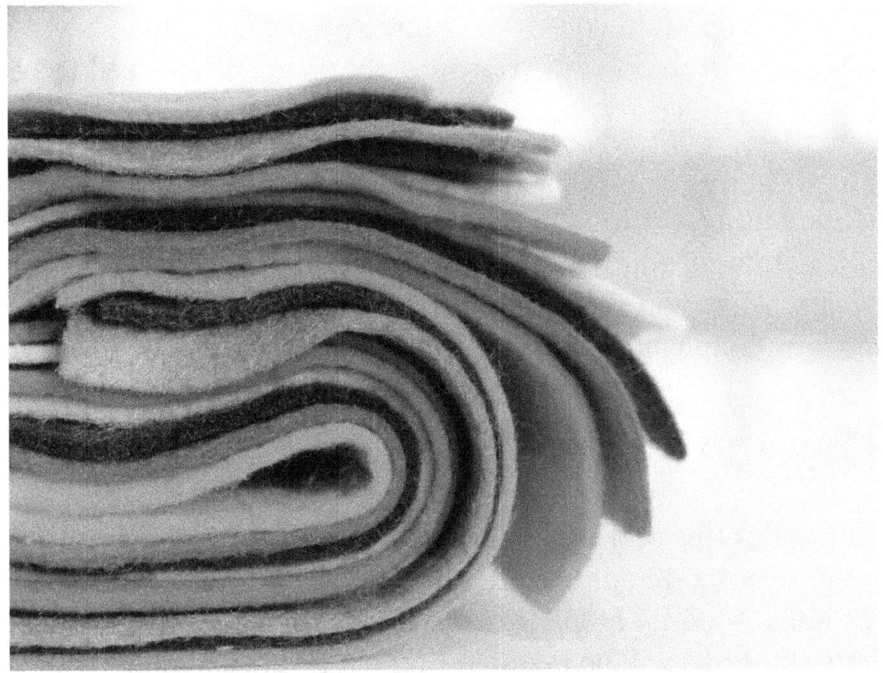

Felt is a fabric that comes in various shapes, sheets, and rolls. Most people are very familiar with felt because it is used in childhood crafts and is often the first fabric on which people sew. It is a thick and sturdy fabric, but the felt that you are familiar with is most likely synthetic. There is nothing wrong with using synthetic fiber in crafts, and your project will turn out nicely if you use synthetic wool or cotton in needle felting. The main difference is the textures. Pure wool and cotton feel softer and slightly springy, whereas synthetic fibers feel more dense.

Felting Knitted Goods

Sometimes knitters felt their finished products by using hot water in the washing machine to agitate their fibers. Needle felting is similar, except you are using a needle to work the fibers instead of hot water. Also, you do not have to knit the initial product! If you are a knitter, you will enjoy having another craft to do with your wool, but you do not need to be a knitter—or crafty in any way—to learn and enjoy needle felting.

While felting a complete knitted product changes the texture of the item, needle felting gives you more freedom with your design. After you create the texture, you can shape the wool into anything you want!

Tips and Tricks

This list of tips and tricks can help you before you get started needle felting. Keep these in mind while you learn. This book includes step-by-step processes for each craft, so the important tips will be restated in the relevant sections.

Make It Firm

Keeping pieces firm is a key part to creating a successful 3D needle felting project. Since the wool fibers are soft, they will spring back when you press them in, but the overall felted piece will be firm.

Roll It Tightly

One of the beginning steps of most projects is to roll loose wool felting into a ball or cylinder before you use a needle on the fibers. The tighter you roll the wool fibers, the easier it will be to complete your project because the core of your sculpture will already be firm.

Tie a Knot

Another way to get a tight, firm core is to tie a knot in the center of your fibers before you start to roll it up.

Make Short Motions

Needle felting requires you to make short stabbing motions into the wool. You do not need to stab the needle all the way through the wool and into your foam pad work station.

Rotate the Piece

As you are needle felting a piece of wool, make sure you keep rotating the piece while you work. If you keep turning the wool, you will be sure to evenly felt the material. Keeping your work in motion will also keep "dimples" from making your final product look uneven.

Start with Less

While many patterns will tell you how much wool roving to use for each step, it is always a good idea to start with less. You cannot take wool away from your project once you start felting it, but you can easily add more fiber which can help your piece get bigger and thicker.

Your Shape Will Shrink

After you have fully felted your fibers, the finished product will be about thirty percent smaller than what you started with. This is the ideal change in size, but note that if you overwork your felting and make it as hard as a rock, it will be over seventy-five percent smaller than what you started with! And super hefty on top of that!

Keep Your Needle Straight

Keep your needle straight when you work: straight into the fibers, straight back out of the fibers. Pulling it out at the same angle you pushed it in will prevent your needle from breaking. If you twist or bend your needle while it is tangled in the fibers, the tip will break off, and you cannot safely continue felting wool if there is a sharp needle embedded in it.

Be Patient

Learning a new skill takes time, and needle felting is no exception. Since you are making stabbing motions with a sharp barbed needle, you will want to be incredibly careful with your work, even if this means starting slow.

You might get frustrated because, as you are working on it, your project does not look like you think it should. The wool roving mostly looks like a mess of fiber, even if you have felted it into a smooth shape. It is not until the final steps of a project when you are putting everything together that you will finally be able to tell your hard work has paid off.

Practice Makes Perfect

The projects in this book will take you step-by-step through the needle felting process. They will provide you with the instruction that you need as you learn general needle crafting skills and discover how they can all work together to make beautiful and adorable projects. That being said, finishing this book will not make you a master fiber artist. There is nothing wrong with practicing the same craft from this book multiple times before moving on to the next. Even if you go through every project once, coming back through to do them all again will be great practice and will definitely improve your needle felting skills. Hopefully the projects in this book will also serve as jumping off points and inspire you to create your own patterns!

Chapter 2:

Needle Felting Equipment

Recently needle felting has become a very popular craft because it is so easy to learn. It does not hurt that the finished product is very cute! To get started with needle felting, you will need some basic equipment.

Basic Equipment

This basic equipment is a must-have to begin needle felting. You will also learn about some different tools and textiles that you might want to try after you complete a few practice projects.

1. Notched Needle

You need a special needle to complete needle felting crafts. Notched needles are the standard tool used. Notched needles have been used as far back as 1859, when they were used in needle punch machines to make batting for blankets. These needles have small notches, or barbs, along the shaft and tip. These barbs grab the fibers when you stick the needle into the wool, tangle it up, and leave it stuck in your shape even as you pull the needle back out. The more you poke the fibers with the notched needle, the stiffer it will become.

To get started with needle felting, you can use a standard notched needle and easily complete the basic crafts. There are four different types of felting needles you might want to use as you become more skilled, but any notched needle will work nicely for beginners.

Felting needles are sharp, so you will want to be careful and pay close attention to your finger placement as you work. Although not a basic supply, finger shields are available if you are worried about stabbing yourself. These are like flexible rubber thimbles that you can wear over your fingers to protect them from the needle. Since they are rubber, they will still allow you a range of movement as you work.

2. Unspun Wool Fleece

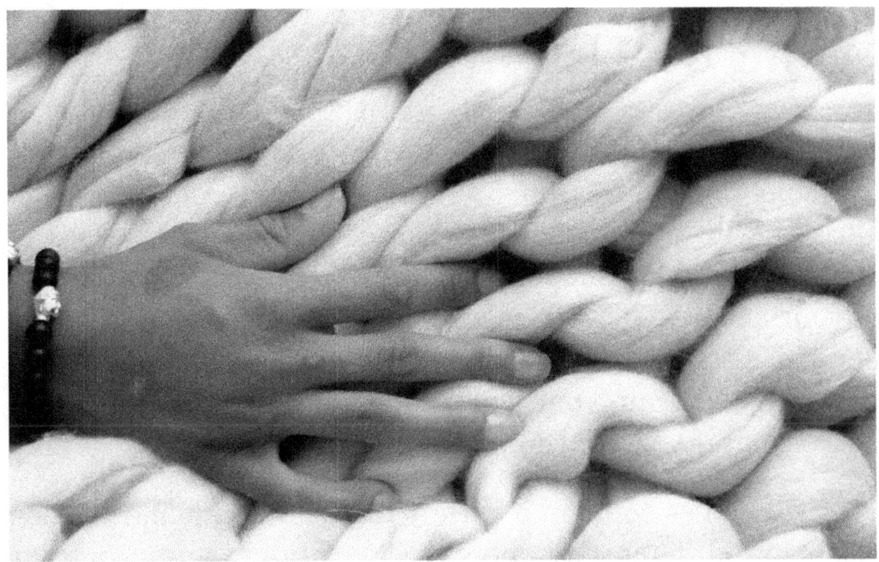

Unspun wool fleece can be found in two styles: roving and batts. Roving means the fibers have been brushed to all run in the same direction so that they are smooth. Batts are sheets of thick wool that have fibers going in all different directions.

Both roving and batts can be used for needle felting. For a beginner, batts are easier because the fibers are already somewhat tangled. You will be able to needle felt a bit and quickly see how the process works and get an idea of what your final product will look like.

3. High Density Foam

High density foam is necessary for your work area when needle felting. Since the needles poke through the wool, they can not hit a hard surface or they will break. You also do not want to use a standard pillow or cushion, because you will get holes in it. Using high density foam will protect your needle from breaking while also preventing needle damage to work surfaces.

Felting Needles

Felting needles are sturdy, and are made to tangle wool fibers into something more firm. Still, you must be considerate when working with your needle. Make sure to always pull it back out at the angle you pushed it in so that you will not break the tip of your needle. This will ensure that your needles last longer, and will also keep you from getting hurt. If the tip of a needle has broken off into your wool, you will either have to extract it—very carefully!—or scrap the entire piece and start again.

Felting needles come in a variety of styles and lengths. They also have different numbers and positions of notches, or barbs, on the shaft of the needle. These notches are what agitate the wool when you stick in your needle, so the number that you have will affect how much work you will have to do to get the wool to the desired texture.

To begin a felting project, you will want to use longer and thicker needles because they will go further into the wool. This, along with innumerable notches on the shaft, will help the needle to catch and tangle more fibers.

Once your wool is tangled, it will be harder to push the thick needle into the fibers. At this point, you can switch to a finer needle so that the work will not be hard, but you will still be able to create texture and volume in your fibers.

Needles with delicate tips have notches close to the point. These are used to smooth out your project when you are on the final steps. This will also make your project look less fuzzy. On the other hand, if you want your sculpture to look fuzzy, there are needles that will give it that appearance.

1. Triangle

Triangle needles have three sides or edges.

2. Star

Star needles have four sides or edges.

3. Twisted/Spiral

Twisted or spiral needles are actually triangular in shape, but they feature a twisted blade to agitate the wool fibers in different ways than the triangle and star needles.

4. Reverse

Reverse needles are the type that will make your finished product look fuzzier. These needles have opposite notches that pull fibers out of your work to make it look fuzzy and fluffy.

Once you see some of the projects that you will be making, you will understand why some sculptures might benefit from a fluffy finish.

Needle Gauges

Felting needles come in different gauges, typically 32, 36, 38, 40, and 42 gauge. Needles with low numbers are thicker, and can be used on coarse wool and to get your projects started. Needles with higher number gauges are thinner, which means that you can use them once your wool fibers are tangled or when you need to do more detailed work.

Felting Needle Pens

Felting needle pens are not for writing—they are tools that hold up to three needles at once. Using multiple needles at the same time makes the felting process incredibly efficient. Once you become more confident with needle felting, you can even create your own version of this tool by combining several needles together. You can attach them with string, wire, or hot glue.

These pens have a sturdy grip attached so you can hold them firmly. Many needle felting pens also have a protective plastic case around the needles. This case gets pushed up when you are working and comes back down automatically when you pull back from the fiber.

Another tool that you might be interested in trying that is called a "clover tool." This tool can hold one, two, or three needles while you work. A benefit to using this tool over a premade felting needle pen is that you can change out the needles. While thicker needles are used at the beginning of a project to quickly agitate more fibers, you will need to use thinner needles as the project progresses. If you are using a felting needle pen, you will need to stop using the pen at a certain point and start to use a more delicate needle. But the clover tool allows you to change out needles so that you can use the tool until you get to the final detail work of your project.

Keep in mind that felting needle pens and homemade tools that use multiple needles are best used at the start of a project. The multiple needles will make quick work of a large flat piece, the body of an animal, or the foundation of a sculpture. As you get into more detailed work, you will need to work with just one needle, and eventually use a higher gauge needle to finish it off.

Best Needle for Needle Felting

As you become a more skilled needle felter, you will be able to choose from a variety of needles according to your craft level, your project, and the stage of your work. For beginners, a 38 gauge needle in the best choice. Within that gauge, you can pick either a spiral or triangular needle. This standard needle will help you to complete the projects in this book as well as many that you, yourself, will create. Pick a needle with a high number of notches because this will make your work more efficient. As a beginner, it is rewarding to be able to see the fruits of your labor quickly, instead of doing a lot of work with a less notched needle and getting frustrated at the lack of progress.

If you purchase a needle felting kit, it might come with a variety of needles. Even if you do not get an entire kit, you can buy a pack of needles—this is an affordable option which not only provides you with different needles but replacements for broken needles. Unfortunately, you will probably break a few no matter how careful you are with your work. The notches on the needles will also wear off over a long period of usage, rendering them ineffective.

Needle Felting Wool

There are many different fibers that you can use for needle felting. Most crafters use wool from sheep, but other fibers, such as those from other animals, plants, and even synthetic fibers, also work well. Even wool from sheep comes in a lot of varieties, depending on the breed of sheep from which the wool is shorn. Breeds include Merino, Icelandic, Wensleydale, Shetland, Romney, New Zealand, Corriedale, Norwegian Lincoln, Herdwick and more. Each of these wools have different textures that you will learn about later. Different textures mean that they will work differently with the notched needles.

Wool is described with microns, with the higher micron rating the coarseness of the fibers. How coarse the natural fibers are will impact how much you will have to work the fibers to adequately felt them. Once it is shorn from the animal, wool can be processed in different ways. These processes might also affect how the fibers can be felted. Over time, you will work with different fibers and discover which ones work best for your style.

1. Short Fiber Wool

Short fiber wool is the best type of textile to use as a beginning needle felter. Since the fibers are short, they are easier to work into a fabric. Since the fibers are coarse and uncombed, this is the best wool to use for the center of your sculptures—it is actually sometimes called "core wool." The coarse fibers work into a sturdy core that will support the additional felted elements that you add to your projects.

Short fiber wool is cheaper than finer wool, which is another plus for beginning crafters! It can be tough to sink a lot of money into a hobby you are not sure you will enjoy, so using short fiber wool to get started is an affordable option.

Short fiber wool comes in a batt, a loose sheet, or a roving. Batts or loose sheets are most likely the easiest way to get started with needle felting, as the roving is a loose rope that some might find intimidating.

2. Long Fiber Wool

Long fiber wool comes combed so the fibers are all running in the same direction. It will look smooth when you purchase it. You can use this for needle felting projects without much trouble, but it is not the best choice for beginners. Since long fiber wool is so smooth, it takes a lot more needle agitation to get the fibers tangled together. It will take more time and effort to get these fibers felted, and that can be discouraging for beginners.

Because long fiber wool is so smooth and is high quality, it is a great fiber to use for more advanced needle felting projects. It comes in a variety of natural and dyed colors, so it is the optimal choice for special projects that you want to use as showpieces, sell, or give as gifts.

3. Wool From Different Breeds of Sheep

Wool from different breeds of sheep felts differently, so you must consider what type of wool you need for your project before you get your supplies.

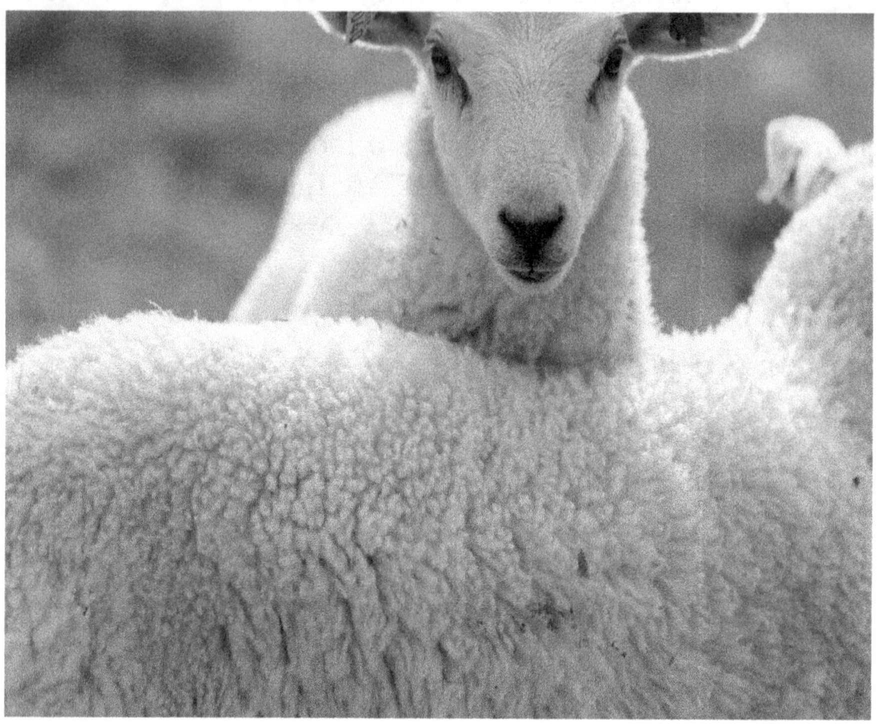

Merino

Merino wool has a fine-medium texture, so it will take more work to properly felt. Once it is done, your project will look smooth.

Icelandic

Icelandic wool is coarse and hairy. Keep in mind that the undercoat felts better than the outer coat.

Wensleydale

Wensleydale wool is unique because it has wavy fleece. This is a great wool to use for animals with long hair, or if you are felting a person or a doll with curly hair.

Shetland

Shetland wool is medium-coarse, but some of the coarse fibers are incredibly difficult to felt. You may wish to wait until you have more experience before using this wool.

Romney

Romney wool is medium-coarse and therefore ideal for needle felting. Some Romney wool is also very soft, so it can be a good option for making stuffed animals or dolls.

New Zealand

New Zealand wool is medium-coarse so it is great for needle felting projects. It is easy to use, but the finish will not look as smooth as a Merino wool project will look.

Corriedale

Corriedale wool is also medium-coarse, so it is a great wool to use as you get started with needle felting.

Norwegian Lincoln

Norwegian Lincoln wool is medium-coarse, so it is an ideal option for needle felting. This type of wool is more coarse than Merino wool and Corriedale wool, if you are caught trying to decide between the three.

Herdwick

Herdwick wool is incredibly coarse, so it is a good wool to use for felting projects.

4. Wool From Other Animals

For unique needle felting projects, consider using wool from other animals. Alpacas, llamas, camels, angora goats, and rabbits all produce fibers that you can use for needle felting. You can even use fur from your pet dogs and cats if you integrate it into other fibers!

Alpacas

The younger the alpaca, the softer the fiber. Texture and length also depend on the part of the alpaca from which the fur is gathered. The blanket fur comes from the main part of the body, between the hind end and neck. This fiber is long and soft. Fur from the neck and upper legs is soft but short, while fiber from the lower legs and belly is fairly coarse.

Llamas

Llama fibers are very soft and delicate. Llamas do not produce much wool, so this rare fiber is rarely used for needle felting.

Camels

Camel fiber is very soft, with tiny natural curls in the texture. When mixed with other wools, the camel fibers will stand out and make a pattern.

Goats

Fiber from angora goats is called mohair and is very shiny. Kid mohair is soft and curly. Yearling fur is more coarse, and wavy instead of curly. This fiber is rated at about 20 microns, meaning that it is fairly soft, though it gets coarser with age.

Rabbits

Angora rabbits also produce soft fur that can be used for needle felting.

Best Wool for Needle Felting

With so many different wool fibers available for crafting, you will want to consider what is best for needle felting. Fine wool is softer to work with, but will take much more time and effort to felt into an attractive sculpture or project. Coarse wool is easier to agitate with notched needles, so you will be able to see the results of your work quickly.

There are wools that are medium-coarse, which is a good middle ground between fine and coarse wool. Medium-coarse wool fibers are easy for the notched needle to grab and agitate, but your final product will still have a smooth finish.

To complete the projects in this book, you will only need a few colors of medium-coarse wool. However, if you want to have a lot of colors on hand so that your creativity can run wild, it is possible to buy kits that have small bundles of many different colors.

Additional Supplies

These supplies are not at all necessary for needle felting. Even the most professional fiber artists might not use these tools, but they are options worth knowing about, because they do influence your work and change how your projects can look.

Carding Brushes

Carding brushes are wire brushes with fine bristles that can be used to smooth and mix wool roving. Hand carders are brushes on a long handle, so you can keep a better grip on them as you work with your fibers. In a pinch, you can use clean pet brushes, because the wire bristles are about the same quality.

Carding brushes use the wire "teeth" to grip fibers that you want to merge together. You use two of these brushes at once, with one color of wool roving in the bristles of one brush, and another color of wool roving in the bristles of the other brush. You gently combine these hand carders so that the wools blend together. This will give you natural highlights in your wool. It is also a great way to get variegated colors of wool roving for certain needle felting projects.

Once the wool has been successfully combined, you can carefully extract it from the bristles of the hand carders and use it just as you would any other wool roving.

Fabric Shavers

You might think that fabric shavers are just for getting pills off of your sweaters and winter coats, but they work wonders in providing the finishing touches on many needle felted items. When you finish a piece of needle felting, you might have some fibers still sticking out of your item. This might be a good look, if you are creating a furry animal! But if you want a smooth felted ball to make stylish jewelry, then you can trim these pesky fibers with a small fabric shaver to give your craft a smooth, sophisticated finish.

Chapter 3:

Getting Started

Learning the basics of needle felting will set you up for success with future projects. If you have never done needle felting before, this is the perfect first project for you. If you have tried needle felting, this is a great project to practice your skills and get in the right mindset for the more involved projects that will come later.

To get started, you will try the basic movements of needle felting to make a heart.

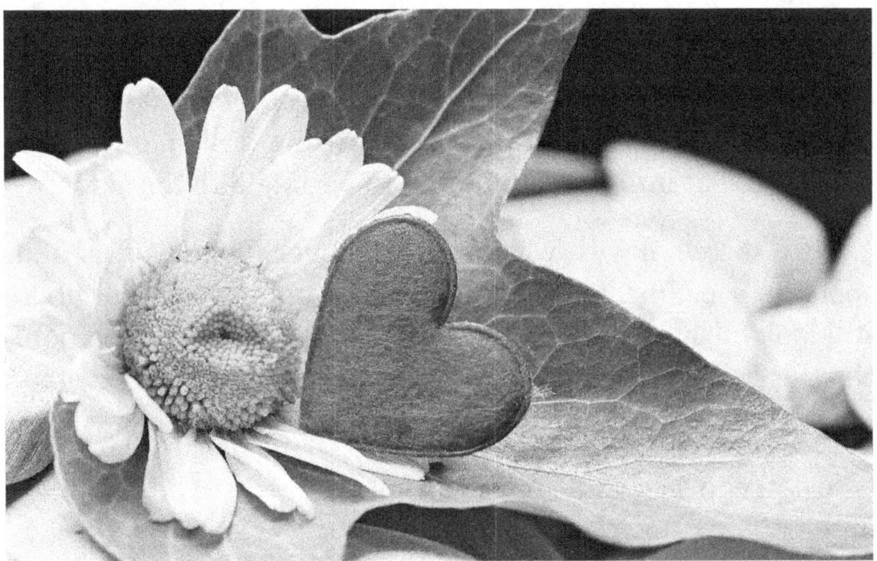

Materials Required

1. One or two felting needles

2. Wool fiber (red color)

3. Foam cushion (for base)

4. Straight pins

Steps to Follow

1. Take your red wool and tear a thick sheet of it. Hold the edges of the roving and pull so you are tearing from the center. Make sure what you tear off is at least ½ inch more than your planned size, because the fibers are longer than your finished, matted project will be. You will always need more wool fiber than you think you will because the fibers get tangled up and become shorter.

2. Lay the torn wool on the foam to start working on it. Be considerate of what you are using as a base for your needle felting. You can use a regular cushion as a base, but you will end up with a lot of holes in it! Foam cushions are firmer so they provide a sturdy work space, while still allowing the needles to get into the foundation to best agitate the wool.

3. Poke the wool with your needle all over. Poke any random spot you see. Just start poking at the wool. If the wool fibers still look fairly smooth, you need to work on them some more. Get the fibers very tangled before moving on to the next step.

4. Use the straight pins to outline the shape of the heart. This is so you can see what shape the felting needs to be; outline it in the way that works best for you.

5. Tuck the excess wool into the middle of the shape, and work it again with the felting needle. Poke it all over so the fibers get tangled together to hold this heart shape.

6. Compress the center of the shape. You want to make sure it will hold together on its own.

7. Fold the excess wool in the center. Agitate the fibers so they grab each other to hold tight.

8. When you turn over the heart, you will see a bunch of fuzzies from where your needle poked through the wool into your foam mat. You can work to gently needle felt these fibers back into the opposite side of the heart. This will smooth it out.

Look at your sweet red heart! Your first basic shape is ready. You have needle felted your first project, and now you know the process.

Chapter 4:

Advancing Your Shape

After making the flat heart shape, you understand the basics of how needle felting works, and how it feels to tangle the fibers together and create shapes that hold together. In this chapter, you will learn how to create advanced shapes. You will needle felt different parts that will be put together to create a sculpture.

You will also learn the concept of using different color wools. Different elements of the sculpture will be different colors, and you will combine the colors and parts to make one cohesive sculpture.

For this needle felting practice, you will be following a step-by-step process to make this adorable cartoon character.

Materials Required

1. Felting needles

2. Different colors of wool

3. Foam base

Steps to Follow

1. First, rip off a piece of wool. Remember to make sure that it is slightly bigger than you want your sculpture to be. This first piece of wool is for the body of the sculpture, so you want to get enough wool to make a firm core.

2. Use this wool to create the body of the sculpture. Agitate the wool until it is firm. Keep rolling more wool into the body in even layers so that it will be sturdy.

3. Next, you will create the belly of the character. Take a bit of the white wool and felt it into an oval shape. Keep this somewhat flat, because you will be sticking it onto the body that you have already created. The white wool is more to give definition to the character than to give it more volume. When you get the white wool into a nice oval shape, use your needle to felt it onto the body.

4. The next step is to create the eyes with small pieces of black wool. You will just need a tiny bit of black fibers for this step, and you will carefully felt it into small circles. Be very aware of your fingers as you work on this small scale!

If you do not feel confident enough in your felting skills to work with something so small, you can cut little circles of flat black felt to use as eyes. Just be aware that synthetic sheets of felt are most likely shinier than the wool you are using for the rest of your sculpture. This will make your character's eyes look different than the rest of your hand made craft.

After you have your eyes, carefully attach them to your character's head by using your notched needle to tangle the fibers together.

5. Your character needs some ears! Take more of the wool that you used for the body, and felt two ear shapes. Leave a bit of stray wool hanging from the ears so you can use your notched needle to push these fibers into your character's head to attach them.

6. Last, but not least, your character needs feet to stand on. Use the same color of wool that you used for the body—or if you want your character to wear shoes, pick another color to use.

Felt thick egg shapes for the feet, and make them firm enough so that you can sculpt them by hand. It might take more agitation than you have used previously, so keep working. Pause every so often to test the texture of the feet. Once you can mold them into shapes, you can flatten the bottom side of it so your character will be able to stand. Make the feet or shoes look however you would like.

Add some wool fiber to the top of the shoes or feet, and felt a little of it into the shoes. Leave some to felt back into the body of your character so that it can stand on its own two feet!

You have made your first sculpture! Now you have got down all of the basic skills needed for needle felting, so you are ready to progress to the next level.

Chapter 5:

Skill Improvement

You have now made a flat needle felted shape and a 3D sculpture. Although the method of making a sculpture is quite different from making a flat shape, all of the basic skills are the same. You make the same motions with the needle whether your product is flat or 3D. Even attaching pieces to a sculpture body involves the same needle movements.

In needle felting, your end result is highly dependent on which material you use and how you use it. There are a few things to take into consideration while needle felting, as these factors will affect your workflow. They will make you more efficient, improve your performance, and elevate the quality of your work.

Improve Your Needle

For the first two projects, only a standard notched needle was needed. However, to be more efficient, you can use a needle felting pen, or create your own version by attaching two or three needles together. Every time you insert them into the wool, they will be working double or triple time for you!

Using different gauges of needles will also help to step up your needle felting game. Thicker needles are great for starting projects, whether you use them alone or as a needle felting pen. But the more you work the fibers, the finer of a needle you will need to be able to make a difference in the felting. Using a more delicate needle will also prevent your needle tip from breaking off when it is forced in.

Using a reverse needle is also a fun way to change up your felting style. Remember, this is the needle that has notches that are the opposite of what the standard needles have. When you use the reverse needle, you will pull out bits of fiber to make your final product look fluffy or fuzzy. This can be a really cute effect to use on animal sculptures!

Vary Your Fiber

So many different types of fiber were defined in Chapter 2 that you should have an idea of what types you might like to work with. There are a variety of coarse fibers that are good for beginners. Medium-coarse fibers will also be easy for beginners to work with.

To step up your needle felting game, try working with medium-fine wools like Merino. Wensleydale is also a great fiber to try, since it is naturally wavy. You can needle felt the ends of some Wensleydale wool into a felted horse sculpture for a flowing mane and tail. You can felt it on the head of a doll or person sculpture for gorgeous locks. Once you experiment with different fibers, your imagination will run wild and help you to figure out what you can create from scratch, or how you can embellish existing patterns.

Incorporate Stitching

You can incorporate stitching on your needle felting projects, whether they are flat or 3D designs.

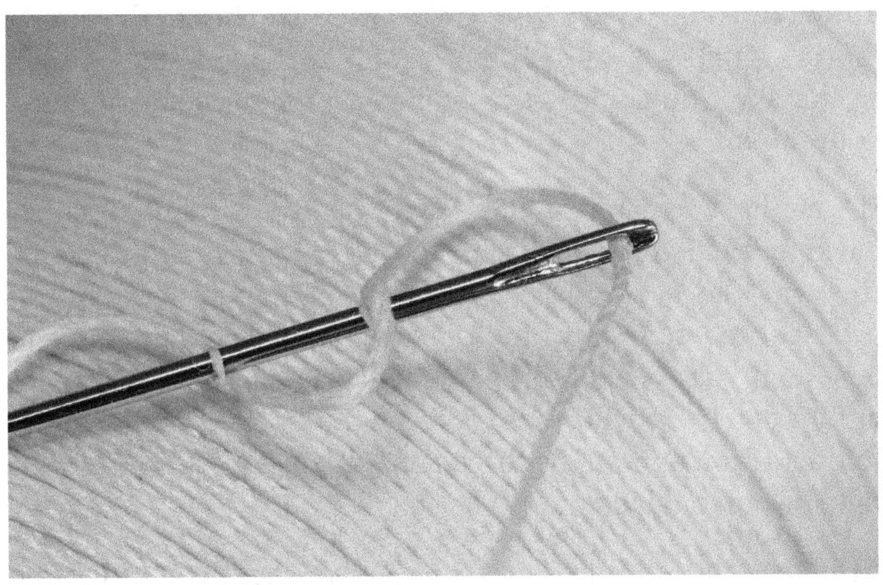

Embroidering Flat Felted Designs

When you are embroidering flat felted designs, you can either stitch directly on the felted wool, or you can put the whole design on a piece of fabric to make a wall hanging or to incorporate into a quilt or larger piece of fabric art.

To make a felted design on fabric, you will felt a flat design just as you did with the heart in Chapter 3. It can be any shape that you choose. Instead of working directly on your foam base surface, put a piece of fabric between your felting project and your foam base. Felting on top of the fabric means your felted design will become attached to the fabric "canvas"! The wool fibers you are felting will become tangled with the fabric. Since the fabric is tightly woven, its fibers will not come loose, but instead will tightly hold the felted material.

Once your felted design has adhered to the fabric, you can add accent colors with embroidery thread by sewing loose stitches around the felted part. You can also add stitches to the empty fabric around your design. For example, if you felted a moon in the sky, you could stitch stars into the area surrounding your moon.

If you have created a flat felted design without a fabric backing, then you can stitch right on the finished project. If this was the heart project from Chapter 3, you could add accent stitches directly onto the heart to make it look broken. Just as if you were outlining your fabric-backed design with embroidery, you will want to keep your stitches loose on the felting. If you tighten the thread too much, it might cause your felted wool to bunch or lose its shape.

Also keep in mind the fact that your stitches go through the entire project, and will be seen on the opposite side of the design. Normally, there is a "bad side" in sewing where all the ends of stitches can be hidden away in a garment's hem, on the inside of work, or beneath the frame. Adding stitches to a flat felting that is meant to stay flat and not mounted to anything means that both sides of the design are visible. There is a way to make the stitching work on both sides, and you can tuck in and trim any loose ends.

Embroidering 3D Felted Designs

You can add stitches to 3D felted designs to give more detail to your work. For example, for the cartoon character you made in Chapter 4, you felted small black eyes to add to the face. If you did not feel comfortable using a felting needle for such small-scale work, you could cut felt circles and attach them to your character's head. However, another option would be to use thread and stitch eyes onto your sculpture. Using embroidery is a great way to level up your needle felted sculptures.

When embroidering a 3D object, you will need to be careful about how deep your needle goes. You will want to keep your stitches shallow and loose so that they do not pull apart the fibers that you have previously felted. If you felted your project to completion, it should be pretty firm, so it will hold stitches well.

Keep in mind that most embroidery thread has a sheen to it. Your felted elements will look soft and fuzzy, but any embroidered accents will be shiny and crisp. This can work well for a project and add a lot of interest, but you will want to take it into consideration in the planning stages. If your finished product would look harsh and surreal with crisp elements added on, you do not want to go through the trouble of adding them and potentially ruining what you have created.

Use Wires and Other Supplies

You can use wire, stuffing, batting, and other supplies to help build your needle felted sculptures.

Wires

There are several ways that you can use wires to your advantage when needle felting. First, you will need to consider the different types of wire, specifically sculpting wire and covered wire. Wires can be used to build a skeleton for your sculptures. They can also streamline your work process so that you have fewer steps necessary to complete your design.

Sculpting Wire

Instead of using short fiber wool as a core for all of your projects, you can use wire to form a base. Think about this step as you are planning your pattern so that you can save on wool. Using wire to form an animal's body will not only save your money and wool, but it will also cut down on the steps needed to complete the project. Instead of having to needle felt a solid ball for the core, you can shape wire and then add layers of felting over it.

There are different gauges of sculpting wire you can use. Thicker wire might require a tool to cut it into the lengths you need, and again to shape it. But this thicker wire will hold its shape, and also be sturdy if you are making a sculpture that will have many layers of felting and additional elements on it. Using thick wire also means your final product will be more durable, so it can be carefully handled and moved around without losing its core structure.

Thinner wire can be cut with regular scissors and is easy to twist into shapes. However, since it is thin and delicate, too many layers of felted wool might weigh it down and push the wire out of the intended shape. If you are doing a light project that will not be handled or moved around too much, thinner wire is a great way to create a skeleton foundation. Thinner wire is also one way to keep limbs slender and proportionate. Instead of having to felt a dense piece of wool for an animal's appendage, you can use wire as the base and just add a light layer of felting over it to keep the visual on point.

This wire can also add flexibility to your project. Needle felter Sara Renzulli is known for her posable needle felted animal sculptures. On her website Sarafina Fiber Art, she has tutorials for how you can use wire to make your animal and people sculptures flexible.

If you are unable to find the exact gauge of wire that you need, consider getting creative and making your own! You can twist together two thinner gauges of wire to make a slightly thicker option. You can even mix a thin and thick gauge of wire together to make a sturdy yet flexible wire skeleton option for your sculpture.

Covered Wire

Covered wire can be used for projects if you need the structure of wire, but do not cover the wire with needle felting. Pipe cleaners are one example of covered wire. They can give your sculpture a sturdy base, because they are strong and flexible. As an added bonus, pipe cleaners are already covered in fuzzy fibers, so they will fit the look of your project.

Pipe cleaners are thin wires twisted together with chenille fibers. They come in a variety of types and lengths. Most pipe cleaners are thin, with bristly chenille fibers sticking out all around the wires. There are also incredibly soft and fluffy chenille pipe cleaners that will be a great addition to luxurious sculptures you might be creating. The wire of these pipe cleaners are typically the same gauge as the thinner kind, but the fibers are longer to give the illusion of fluffiness.

Pipe cleaners come in thicknesses of 4, 6, 9, and 12 mm. Keep in mind that this references the thickness of the fibers, which will impact the overall look, or fluffiness, or your project. This thickness does not refer to the gauge of the wire at the core.

You can find pipe cleaners in a variety of colors, including some that have glitter or metallic accent fibers added in with the chenille. There are also bump pipe cleaners, where the stem will be relatively thin and then fluff up into a larger bump shape on the stem, then go back down to thin. This type of pipe cleaner can be used to add interesting features to your needle felted sculptures!

In addition to pipe cleaners, there are also brands of wire that are covered in fabric or a thin layer of paper. These are smooth wires, compared to the fuzziness of pipe cleaners. For this type of wire, the gauge does refer to the wire itself, since the layer of fabric or paper covering it is very thin. These wires are typically available in 22-, 26-, and 32- gauge.

Covered wire, such as pipe cleaners or fabric covered wire, can also be used as decorative elements in your statues. If your sculpture is a basket, you can braid natural-colored covered wire together to make the woven handle. If your sculpture is holding a bouquet of flowers, you can use green pipe cleaners or green fabric covered wire as the flower stems. Using covered wire in these ways will not only cut down the number of steps in your craft project, but will make it look more polished overall. Making green felt stems will take a lot of small scale needle felting, and it might not look right once you are done. The felted stems would have to be very dense to stand up straight, and the weight of such a bouquet might topple your sculpture! Using green covered wire will prevent your flowers from drooping.

Stuffing

Just as you can use wire to create a structural foundation, you can use stuffing to round out your 3D figures. Stuffing is less expensive than wool fibers, so using rolled up bits of stuffing instead of wool fibers for the core of your sculpture will save you money. It also reserves your wool fibers for bits of the craft that will be seen, instead of hiding the higher quality materials inside of the sculpture. You can even needle felt the cotton or synthetic fibers so that they will be more tangled together, and therefore create a stronger, denser core for your sculpture.

If you are making stuffed animals instead of sculptures, using pillow stuffing at the center of your project will keep it cuddly. If you need something firmer but still soft, you can try quilt batting. The options are limitless, so use your imagination!

Use Cookie Cutters

You can make any flat shape you choose by using straight pins to map out the area you will be felting. If you want to practice set shapes, you can also use cookie cutters. Keep them flat on your foam base and put the wool inside of the cookie cutter. Keep felting it to the edges of the cookie cutter, just as you did with the straight pins.

Cookie cutters are a great option because you have so many choices available to you. If you want to make flat felt shapes, pendants, decorations, or ornaments for a certain holiday, you can just buy a set of cookie cutters! Craft and baking stores will have sets like this available, so you can buy a set of assorted winter shapes, Christmas shapes, Valentines shapes, Thanksgiving shapes, and more.

Cookie cutters also come in general shapes like circles, squares, stars, lightning bolts, and more. Using these cookie cutters will give you the ability to needle felt a variety of shapes that you can then morph into other shapes or even sculptures. You can needle felt a rectangle and a circle and then combine them to make a microphone. You can then leave this as it is, add a hanger so it can be an ornament or a decoration, or make it a pendant for a necklace. You can even felt it onto a piece of fabric and add stitching like explained above.

Or you can take the flat rectangle and add fibers to it until you have made a cylinder. Likewise, you can add fibers to the circle shape until it is a ball, and you can felt it to the cylinder to make a 3D microphone.

Using cookie cutters to make shapes is a great way to practice your needle felting skills, but it is also a good way to find inspiration. Mindlessly making shapes within the borders of a cookie cutter might help you to see some of the things that you could make.

Chapter 6:

Beads

This chapter will give you step-by-step instructions to create beads using needle felting techniques. As Eleanor Stanwood, one of the first needle felting artists, said, using needle felting for jewelry is ideal because wool is a renewable resource, the beads are biodegradable, and they can be composted! Instead of spending money on fast fashion jewelry, making your own needle felted beads is an environmentally friendly way to make unique jewelry.

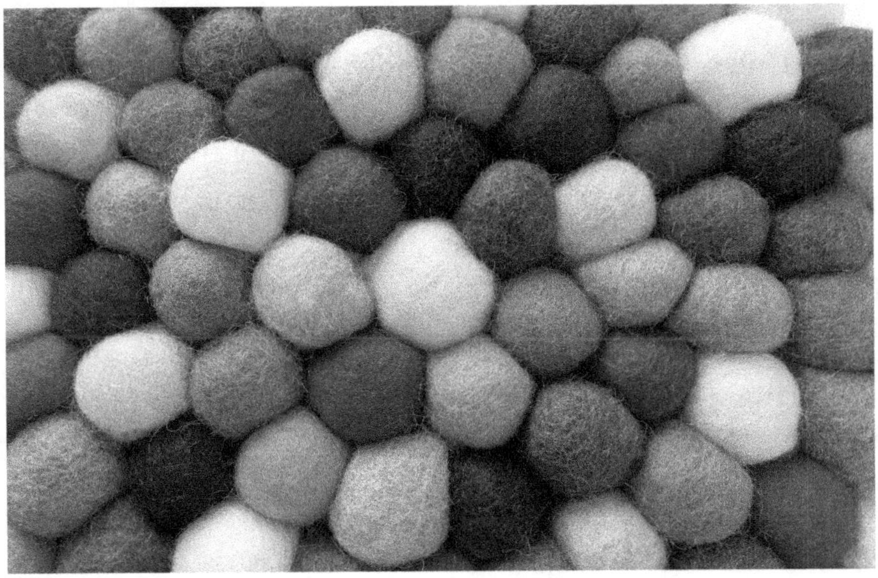

Materials Required

1. Needles

2. Merino wool

3. Foam base

4. Warm water and dishwashing soap

Steps to Follow

1. Mix together the warm water and a squirt of dishwashing soap.

2. Take two tufts of 4 to 5 inches of wool. This much wool will make a bead that is about the size of a small cherry. If you want to make many beads that are all the same size, you might want to consider weighing the tufts so you can ensure your beads will be uniform.

To start with, you will want to choose two tufts of the same wool. Once you see how the bead comes together, you can experiment by choosing two different colors of wool. This will make your bead to have two colors swirled together.

3. Roll one of the tufts of wool very tightly.

4. Place the tightly rolled tuft at a right angle to the bottom of the other tuft.

5. Roll them up together very tightly, starting from the bottom, until you have a rough ball shape.

6. Hold the roll together very tightly, and dip it into the soapy water for a few seconds.

7. Hold the ball in the palm of your hand and add a drop of soap to it.

8. Put the ball between your palms and start to roll it. Do not apply pressure to the ball, as it is malleable in this state and applying pressure will change the shape. You are simply rolling the fibers together, not condensing them into a denser ball.

Once the ball starts to shrink and harden, you can apply a little more pressure to it as you are rolling. This will help it shrink into a felt bead.

9. Rinse the soap off of the bead and let the bead dry. Once it is dry, you can poke a needle through it to make a hole, or thread a needle through it if you know you are going to put it on a string.

The bead will be pretty dense and firm, but since it is made of wool, it will be a little springy and squeezable. Felt beads are slightly fluffy, but you can use a shaver for removing sweater pilling to give it a smoother finish.

You have made a felted bead! This process is called wet felting, and while it is different from needle felting, it is still a hands-on craft. Using soap and water will make the bead firmer when it dries. This method could also be used as part of the process of needle felting a more involved sculpture. Adding soap and water to the body or core of a statue would make it dense and sturdy so that other more traditional needle felting elements may be attached.

Now that you have learned this style of felting, you can experiment with the process and make more beads. Having rolled two tufts of fiber together to create a bead, you can make unique beads. You can also experiment with sizes, using smaller tufts of wool for smaller beads, or larger tufts to make large beads.

After feeling the texture of this first bead, you can change how much pressure you apply to the bead when you are rolling it between your hands. You can apply pressure in different areas of the bead. You could make a long bead by rolling it back and forth in one direction, instead of rolling it all around. Wait until it starts to take shape with the soap and pull out fibers from the ends, making it slightly pointy at each end. When the bead is almost done, you can press each side against a flat, hard surface to make a cube or rectangle. You can flatten your bead into a disc by either applying a great deal of pressure with your hands, or use a hammer to press it flat.

You can embellish the finished bead. Consider using stitching, as was discussed in Chapter 5. You can wrap the beads in wire to give them a caged look, which is very popular in statement necklaces. You can even anchor small beads, sequins, or pearls to the felted beads to completely transform their appearance.

Think of what you would like to make with these felted beads, and that will influence the size that you need to create. You can make enough beads to string together on a necklace or bracelet. You can use the beads like a single charm on a necklace or bracelet. These also make cute key rings and cell phone charms. You can even thread them on a long string and hang them around your house like a garland, or hang them from the ceiling like a mobile. Your designs and jewelry do not have to be made only of felted beads, either. You can alternate jewelry beads with felted beads, use twists of colored wire, or use gold and silver elements to make unique designs that spotlight your felted beads.

Chapter 7:

Mini Teacup Pincushion

You have been using straight pins to outline shapes for flat needle felting projects, but where have you been keeping these pins? This adorable mini teacup pincushion is the perfect way to practice your needle felting while making a practical item to use for your craft supplies. This step-by-step guide will teach you how to make this cute teacup pincushion.

Materials Required

1. 20 grams of Merino wool roving

2. Separate small amounts of Merino wool in different colors for cup decorations and the beverage that will be in the teacup

3. Two 40 gauge triangular needles

4. Foam base

Steps to Follow

1. Take a length of wool roving that measures about 50 x 4 centimeters. This will become your teacup, so use the wool

that you have the most of, and make sure it is one that will allow the embellishment colors to show up nicely.

2. Tease it out gently so that it can lay out to make a flat strip.

3. Roll it up to make a short tube.

4. Use needles to start shaping it like a teacup. Using two needles, or a needle felting pen, will make this step of the process go much quicker. As you are shaping the cup, make sure that you are not just making it a round cylinder. Think of how a teacup looks, and try to squeeze in the bottom of the piece that you are working on. This will give your teacup a smaller base, and will make it look more realistic and delicate.

5. When you have formed the teacup, take a pinch of wool to make a little handle. Remember, this should be the same color as the wool fiber you used to make the teacup so it will form together to make one cohesive item.

6. Shape the bit of wool on your foam first. Think of what a teacup handle looks like and try to mimic that shape. It might be a little difficult since you are working with such a small bit of wool, but the handle can be solid. It does not need to look like a real teacup handle you can put your finger through—those details can be added with embroidery thread before you finalize your project.

While it is still soft, attach your needle felted handle to the cup. Simply felt the loose ends of the handle into the body of the cup.

7. Use one needle to give the handle a fancy shape. Poking the needle into a concentrated area will help stiffen it up and give it a more refined shape than the rest of the handle. This shape can look like a little loop or scroll at the bottom of the handle,

like you might see on fine china. It adds a touch of whimsy to your teacup.

8. Cover the cup with a thin layer of wool. This will help it look smoother, and more like the finish on a teacup (minus the china's sheen) instead of leaving it looking like raw needle felting. Use one needle to finish the surface to achieve the maximum smoothness.

9. Tear off a good bit of wool for the beverage color. Since this is a teacup, you will want to use colors that look like teas, coffee, or hot chocolate.

10. Place the beverage colored wool on top of the cup. Needle felt it into place by winding the wool in a circular direction as you work. This will make it look like a liquid beverage swirling in a cup.

11. Add some surface patterns to the cup itself with different colors of wool. Using pinks, reds, and greens would be a cute way to imply a design of flowers and leaves. You can also simply make patterns of dots or stripes. Keep the needle felting work of this step loose and free, so the fibers will closely resemble hand painted china.

In addition to felting designs on the cup, you could embellish it with beads, gems, or pearls. You could also use embroidery thread to hand stitch designs on the cup instead of needle felting them.

While you are embellishing the cup, use a complimentary color of thread to add stitching along the edge of the handle. This will function like an optical illusion to give details to your handle and make it look more like something you can grab to drink from, instead of looking like a solid handle piece.

12. To make a matching saucer, gently tear a length of roving that measures about 30 x 4 centimeters.

13. Wind it into a circular saucer shape. Begin working on it with both needles so this process will go much quicker. As you needle felt the saucer, continually turn it in your hands so it will get worked into a quality circle. Pinch the edge between your thumb and finger as you work, because this will give your saucer a slightly raised rim and help make it look realistic.

Once your saucer is big enough to compliment your teacup, or about 8 centimeters in diameter, then you need to cover it with a fine layer of wool, just like you did for the teacup. Remember, this will make the saucer look smooth and refined instead of showing the tangle of the felting.

To finish off the saucer, you can needle felt a design that matches the cup, or even just add a simple stitch around the edge like you did with the teacup handle.

Your mini teacup pincushion is ready. You might think that it is so adorable that it would make a good toy, too. Many children would probably love to have a felted teacup for their own tea parties. You could even use this project as a basic pattern, and continue making an entire tea set!

Chapter 8:

Needle Felt Writing

This chapter will give you a step-by-step, in-depth guide to needle felt your name onto a pillow or cushion. Once you learn needle felt writing, you might like to practice by adding people's names to personalized items, or even making beautiful needle felted quotes to hang up as home decor.

Materials Required

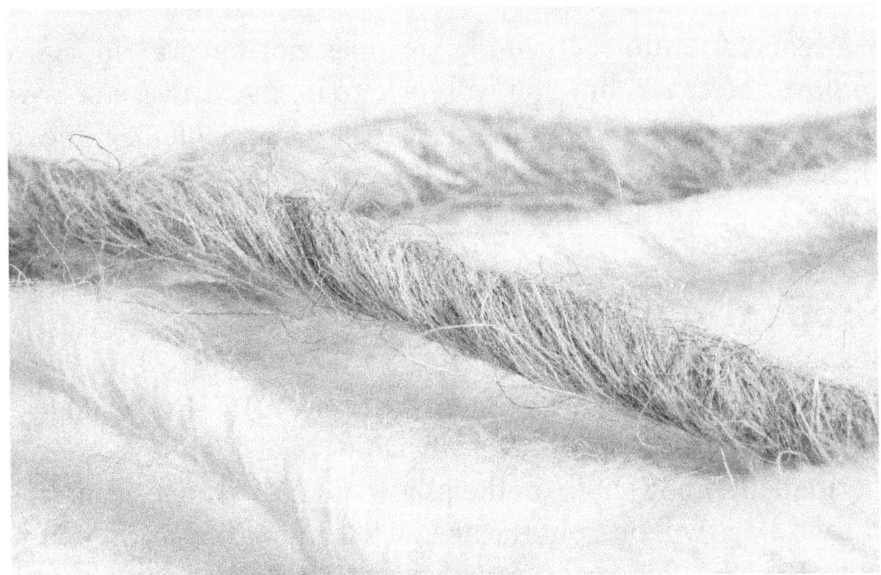

1. Felting wool in one color.

Once you learn needle felt writing, you might be able to do variegated colors across the same word by carefully tucking in one color as you move on to the next. But to learn the basic skills of needle felt writing, it is best to just use one color.

2. Felting Needle

3. Sponge.

This sponge is replacing the foam base you usually use for needle felting projects. The sponge is small enough to fit inside the cushion cover, since you will want to needle felt on only one side of the cushion. If you do not have a sponge in place behind the cushion, your needles will go through both layers of the cover and felt the sides together so that it will be impossible to put over a cushion. As you work, periodically check the sponge to make sure it is still in the right place so that you are only going through one layer of fabric.

4. A cushion or pillowcase on which to felt.

You can felt onto a cushion that does not have a zipper to remove the cover, but you will have to be more aware of how deep your needles are going. If it is at all possible to remove the cushion cover, you will want to do so. You can always use a pillowcase for this practice.

Steps to Follow

1. First iron the pillowcase or cushion cover. If it has wrinkles, you might needle felt over these wrinkles and they will permanently be visible on the pillow. Or, worst case scenario, the wrinkles will pull out the needle felting writing as they ease out. Get your pillowcase ironed as smooth as you can.

2. Write your name on the cushion cover with the pencil. If you mess up, you can rub out the pencil markings or make sure it will be covered with your needle felting in the end. Try to mimic the style or font in which you want your name. If you want it to look like a cursive font, write it that way with a pencil. If you want it to be in all capital letters, write it that way. Making it look exactly how you want with the pencil will make it easier for you once you actually begin felting, because you can just follow your drawn lines.

3. Insert the sponge inside the cover behind the place where you wrote your name. This is the spot where you will be needle felting, and you do not want your needles to go through both layers of pillowcase. Pay close attention to the sponge to ensure it is always behind your work area.

4. Pull out a thin strand of wool from the ball of your chosen color.

5. Place the strand of wool over the first part of your pencil markings. Begin to stab it into the pillowcase with your needle.

6. As you move on to the next letter, add more wool onto your pencil markings. Make sure that your sponge is under your new work area. You will also want to make sure that you are using the same amount of wool for each letter, so it looks like one cohesive word.

6. You can use a needle holder or needle felting pen to use multiple needles at the same time. This will agitate the wool faster so that it will felt onto your pillowcase easily.

Your name is done! Now that you know how to needle felt letters, you can make other designs and decorations, and even try to use several different colors within the same project.

Chapter 9:

Ornaments

In this in-depth, step-by-step guide, you will learn how to create ornaments for the holidays—but you might just want to keep them up year-round and call them home decorations.

Materials Required

1. String that is thin enough to pull through dense felted balls

2. Scissors

3. Wooden beads

4. Embroidery needles

5. Felt balls or pom-poms, which call for wool, water, and liquid soap

Steps to Follow

1. Make felted balls or pom-poms. This part of the project involves the wet felting that we learned in Chapter 6. For these steps, you will need wool in many colors, a small bowl of water, and a few drops of dishwashing soap.

2. Mix together the warm water and a squirt of dishwashing soap.

3. Take two tufts of 4 to 5 inches of wool. This much wool will make a ball that is about the size of a small cherry. For these ornaments, you will want to make many different sized balls, from small to large, in order to have a lot of different decorating options.

4. Roll one of the tufts of wool very tightly.

5. Place the tightly rolled tuft at a right angle to the bottom of the other tuft.

6. Roll them up together very tightly, starting from the bottom, until you have a rough ball shape.

7. Hold the roll together very tightly, and dip it into the soapy water for a few seconds.

8. Hold the ball in the palm of your hand and add a drop of soap to it.

9. Put the ball between your palms and start to roll it. Do not apply pressure to the ball, as it is malleable in this state and applying pressure will change the shape. You are simply rolling the fibers together, not condensing them into a denser ball.

10. As you are rolling the ball and it begins to firm up, you can apply pressure in different ways, and on different parts of the ball, in order to make it different shapes. Think of the shape of some of your favorite ornaments and try to recreate those shapes in your felted balls.

11. Rinse the soap off of the ball and let the balls dry.

12. As the balls dry, gather the rest of your necessary supplies.

13. Plan the overall look of your ornaments by laying them down in order in a straight line. This is the time to play with the design of the ornaments, and mix and match colors. You can make ornaments for specific holidays, or decorations to keep up for entire months or seasons.

You might want to use red and green felted balls to make Christmas ornaments, or blue, white, and grey felted balls for general winter decorations. Orange and black felted balls will look cute for Halloween decor, or you can use orange, yellow, and brown felted balls to make decorations that you can leave up for all of autumn. You can use pastel felted balls for spring, and add egg-shaped beads or pearls in between for extra decoration.

Adding in beads, wood, or other textured elements will make your ornaments and decorations incredibly unique. Play around with the designs and let your creativity guide your process.

14. Measure a string that is three inches longer than double the length of your ornament. Since your designs are laid out in front of you, it is easy to just hold up the string, then fold it back on itself to get double the length of the ornament.

Use a ruler or measuring tape to make sure that you are adding three inches onto that length of string. If you are in doubt, string up to two feet long will be more than enough for your ornament.

15. Insert one end of your string into the eye of your embroidery needle. Make sure you knot the end of the string. If you use a small knot, your first element might fall off of the string. If you use a complimentary color of thread you can knot it around your first felted ball, and it will not be visible on your ornament. If you want to start with a decoration, you can tie a

bead at the end of your string so it will ensure the ornaments will not fall off once you hold them upright.

16. Pass the needle through all the ornaments so the thread combines them all together.

17. Leave a loop above the top element of your ornament. This is how you will hang up your decoration.

18. Thread the string back through all of your felted balls and beads. This will give your ornament an extra sturdy string to hang from. Remember to cut your string so that it is double the length of your ornaments!

19. Tie another knot at the bottom of your ornament. Make sure that it will not pass back through the felted ball. Tie it back around the last bead or ball to be extra safe.

20. Trim off any extra string that is hanging from the final knot on your ornament.

Your ornament is ready to hang up! These are so cute, you may want to leave them up year-round. Although these ornaments are simple to make, they are attractive enough to attach to gifts. They will not only make your gifts look attractive, but your gift recipient will be able to hang the needle felted ornament in their own home—two gifts in one!

Chapter 10:

Cherry Bag Charms

It is hard to believe that this needle felting project is so quick and easy to make, because it looks adorable and professionally done! People will think you bought this purse charm, and will be astonished when you tell them that you made it yourself. In this chapter, you will learn how to create cherry bag charms with step-by-step instructions.

Materials Required

1. Felting wool (natural and red)

2. Felting needle

3. 8" length of leather cord

4. Metal key ring

5. Green felt

6. Foam base

7. Low-temperature hot glue gun

Steps to Follow

1. Fold your leather cord in half and hold it in the middle of the metal key ring.

2. Pull the ends of the leather cord through the loop and secure it into the ring. This will hold your leather cord tight to the metal key ring. You should not need to tie it. If you decide later that you want to take this charm off of the key ring, you can easily pull the leather cord back through the loop.

3. Tie a knot on each end of the leather. At this point, you should have the leather cord looped around the key ring, with two equal lengths of leather hanging down. There should be one knot at the end of each piece of leather cord hanging down.

4. Wrap a long length of the natural colored wool roving around your fingers. It should form a loose ball that is about the size of a golf ball. It will not be dense like a golf ball, though, because you need to make sure there is a hole in the center of the roving.

5. Slip one of the lengths of leather through the middle of the wool roving. You should see the knot sticking out of the end of the wool.

6. Use your hands to shape the natural colored wool into a tighter ball, and then needle felt it to make it as tangled as it can be. When you have finished felting the natural colored roving, it should, of course, be the size of a cherry.

7. To create a second cherry, wrap another long length of the natural colored wool roving around your fingers. Remember that it is a loose ball, about the size of a golf ball. Make sure there is a hole in the center of the roving.

8. Slip the other length of leather through the middle of the wool roving. The knot will be sticking out of the end of the wool.

9. Use your hands to shape the natural colored wool into a tighter ball, and then needle felt it to make it as tangled as it can be. When you have finished felting the natural colored roving, it should be the same size as the first cherry you made.

10. Add a thin layer of red wool fiber over each cherry. Use a needle to secure it onto the natural wool roving. Continue to needle felt the red wool fiber onto the natural colored cherry until it is firmly adhered to the surface. At this stage, it should look like you have two cherries on brown stems, hanging from a key ring. But you are not done yet!

11. Use the green felt to cut out two leaves. If you want to use green wool roving to felt leaves yourself, you can. However, with the leaves being so small, needle felting them yourself would not cause them to look much different than using green felt. The choice is up to you!

Whether you cut leaves from a sheet of green felt or needle felt your own leaves, you will need to hot glue them to the back of your cherry stems. You can loosen the leather loop, hot glue the leaves on, and then tighten the leather loop back over the ends of the leaves. This will not only cover the hot glue, but will provide a little extra security against your leaves falling off.

You have made the cutest cherry purse charm! Now that you see how fun and easy these are to make, you can make many more pairs to spruce up all of your bags and give to friends.

Chapter 11:

Mini Needle Felt Owls

You previously made an animal when you made a cartoon character as your first 3D project in Chapter Four. Hopefully you loved making animals, because in this fun project, you will learn how to create three unique miniature needle felted owls. You will not believe how cute these creatures are!

Materials Required

1. Felting Needles

2. Foam base

3. Low-temperature hot glue gun

4. Wool roving in grey, white, teal, and light teal

5. 2 black beads for eyes for each owl, up to 6 total

6. Foam eggs, one for each owl's body (You can buy these from a craft shop, or shape your own from larger blocks of foam or styrofoam)

Steps to Follow

Owl Option #1

1. Wrap the grey roving around the foam egg. Use the felting needle to poke the wool into the foam repeatedly. Keep agitating the wool fibers until the felt is smooth.

2. Working on the foam base, use the light teal wool roving to create a heart shape. This was the first project that you learned to do in Chapter 3, so you might need to refer back to those instructions. Remember that you can shape a heart by using straight pins as an outline, or even by using a heart-shaped cookie cutter as your border. If you are using straight pins as a border, you might consider leaving them in place if you want to make all three versions of the owl, because you will be making a heart shape again.

After agitating the light teal felt into a firm heart shape, make sure that the felt is smooth.

3. Place the light teal heart shape on the grey body. Poke the heart shape into the grey felt over and over until it is smooth and adheres completely to the egg shape.

4. Take the small black beads and use your low-temperature glue gun to stick each bead into place on the owl's heart-shaped face.

5. Now is the time to customize your owl! You can use embroidery thread to stitch on a little teal beak below your owl's eyes. You can also use the teal thread to make little stitches on your owl's chest that will look like feathers.

Owl Option #2

This foundation for this owl will be created much like the first owl was made, but other elements will be used to make this creature look unique.

1. Wrap the light teal roving around the foam egg. Use the felting needle to poke the wool into the foam repeatedly. Keep agitating the wool fibers until the felt is smooth.

2. Using the foam base as your work station, take a length of white wool roving and tangle it into an oval. This will be a cute white belly for your owl, so after you felt it a bit, hold it up to your light teal felted egg and make sure the size looks right for a belly.

If you need to make it larger, you can add more white wool fibers while you are felting. If your white belly oval is too large, start folding in some of the excess fibers around the edge. Working from the edge towards the center will help you to keep the oval shape, but will also make it smaller.

3. Place the white felted oval onto the light teal egg-shaped body. Make sure that you get it into the perfect position, and needle felt the white oval onto the egg.

4. Working again on the foam base, use the teal wool roving to create a heart shape. This is how you made the face for your first owl back in Chapter 3, so you can refer back to those instructions if you need to. You can shape a heart the same way you did for your first owl: by using straight pins as an outline or a heart-shaped cookie cutter as your border.

After agitating the teal felt into a firm heart shape, make sure that the felt is smooth.

5. Place the teal heart shape on top of the white belly. Depending on the size of your white oval, you might need to have the teal heart overlapping from the white oval onto the grey body.

Poke the heart shape into the white felt (and grey felt, if necessary) over and over until it is smooth and adheres completely to the belly and egg shape.

6. Take the small black beads and use your low-temperature glue gun to stick each bead into place on the owl's heart-shaped face.

7. Now you can further customize your second owl! You can use embroidery thread to stitch on a little beak below your owl's eyes. Consider using grey thread for this owl's beak, since the face is made of the vibrant teal. Use the teal thread to make little stitches on your owl's white belly to look like feathers.

Owl Option #3

This foundation for this owl will be created much like that of the first owl, but other elements will be used to make this creature look unique. This is the most involved owl design, so save it until last as will you have practiced your skills with the first two owls.

1. Wrap the grey roving around the foam egg. Use the felting needle to poke the wool into the foam repeatedly. Keep agitating the wool fibers until the felt is smooth.

2. Using the foam base as your work station, take a length of white wool roving and tangle it into an oval. This will be a cute white belly for your owl, so after you felt it a bit, hold it up to your grey felted egg to make sure that the size looks right for a belly.

If you need to make it larger, you can add more white wool fibers in while you are felting. If your white belly oval is too large, start folding in some of the excess fibers around the edge. Working from the edge in will help you keep the oval shape, but will work to make it smaller in the process.

3. Place the white felted oval onto the grey egg-shaped body. Make sure that you get it into the perfect position, and needle felt the white oval onto the egg.

4. Use a long strip of light teal wool roving and keep working on your foam base. Felt the strip so it makes a somewhat thick length of rope. Hold it up to your owl and see if the light teal rope can completely outline the white belly. You need it to be this long, and then add in a bit extra length for this owl's unique beak.

5. Once your light teal rope of needle felting is long enough, needle felt it all around the white belly as a border. Start from the top, and needle felt it into place in a clockwise direction. When you get back to the top of the owl's head, you should still have a bit of the light teal felt left. Go straight down the owl's forehead to make a beak. Work the remaining bit of the light teal roving into a flat circle on the owl's face.

6. Take the small black beads and use your low-temperature glue gun to stick each bead into place on the owl's face, putting one on each side of the light teal felting nose.

7. Now you can further customize your owl! You can use light teal embroidery thread to make little stitches on your owl's white chest to look like feathers.

Your owls are ready. It is incredible how different the same base project looks with just a few tweaks or even alternate colors of wool. You can use these three owls to make cute woodland scenes as decorations or tablescapes.

Chapter 12:

Button Making

While most of the projects you have learned so far have been cute decorations, this chapter will teach you how to make something very practical! With step-by-step instructions, you will learn how to create a button using needle felting.

Materials Required

1. Felting needle

2. Wool roving, any color

3. Embroidery thread, color matching your roving

4. Foam base

Steps to Follow

1. Take a piece of wool roving in your choice of color. Loosely shape it into a flat disc about 2 centimeters thick.

2. Round out your roving and fold it in from the edges so that it has a diameter of about 5 centimeters.

3. Agitate the wool fibers with your notched needles. Felt the button until it has tightened up to be about a third of the size you started with.

4. As you felt the button, hold the edges between your thumb and first finger. This will create a slight rim on the edge of the button. Leave the cup shape in the middle. Even if it seems like a deep cup, it will equal out when you add the finishing touches.

5. Keep felting the button until it has reduced down to your desired size.

6. Using a standard needle, poke four holes in the center of your button. You do not want to use a felting needle for this step, because the notches will pull out some fibers from the holes. Having loose fibers around the button holes will make it difficult to see the holes to sew on your button.

7. Now you can use this craft as a button on clothing, make it into jewelry and pins, or wear it as a brooch.

This button has a diameter of 3.5 centimeters, with a thickness of 1.5 centimeters. Once you see the finished size of this button, you can make more buttons at this size, to keep them uniform for a garment, or you can try to make some even smaller, depending on the item of clothing on which you want to add buttons. To make smaller buttons, you can use a bit less wool roving, or simply felt the fibers even more tightly so that they will stay together.

If you use this pattern to make buttons for clothes, remember to hand wash these garments. Washing the buttons in hot water or in a washing machine will wet felt the wool, making the buttons shrink up and get even firmer!

Chapter 13:

Felted Ball Earrings

In this chapter, you will learn how to create stylish felted ball earrings.

Materials Required

1. Felting needles

2. Wool roving in at least three different colors

3. Jewelry pliers

4. Large needles

5. Jewelry wire

6. Two earring hooks

7. Foam base

8. Bowl of water

9. Liquid dishwashing soap

Steps to Follow

1. Mix together the warm water and a squirt of dishwashing soap.

2. Take two tufts of 4 to 5 inches of wool. This much wool will make a bead that is about the size of a small cherry.

3. Roll one of the tufts of wool very tightly.

4. Place the tightly rolled tuft at a right angle to the bottom of the other tuft.

5. Roll them up together very tightly, starting from the bottom, until you have a rough ball shape.

6. Hold the roll together very tightly, and dip it into the soapy water for a few seconds.

7. Hold the ball in the palm of your hand and add a drop of soap to it.

8. Put the ball between your palms and start to roll it. Do not apply pressure to the ball, as it is malleable in this state and applying pressure will change the shape. You are simply rolling the fibers together, not condensing them into a denser ball.

Once the ball starts to shrink and harden, you can apply a little more pressure to it as you are rolling. This will help it shrink into a felt bead.

9. Rinse the soap off of the bead and let the bead dry. Once it is dry, you can poke a needle through it to make a hole, or thread a needle through it if you know you are going to put it on a string.

The bead will be pretty dense and firm, but since it is made of wool, it will be a little springy and squeezable. Felt beads are slightly fluffy, but you can use a shaver for removing sweater pilling to give it a smoother finish.

10. Repeat steps 1 through 9 until you have six beads made. You should have two beads of each color so you can make a matching set of earrings.

11. Take the jewelry wire and thread it through the eye of your large needle. You need to fold up the end of the wire so the balls do not fall off when you hold it upright. You can fold the wire into a small, square, or hammer it down to a flat base, like the head of a nail.

12. Lay out your felted balls in the order you want them on your earrings. This might mean that you let them dangle from smallest down to largest. You might have a preference on color order. Laying out your designs first gives you a chance to imagine how they will look as completed earrings, so this is your chance to test out every option.

13. Push the needle and jewelry wire through the first felted ball. If you want to add beads or other embellishments between each felted ball, make sure to add it here.

14. Push the needle and jewelry wire through the second felted ball. If you added beads or other embellishments after the first felted ball, make sure to add one here.

15. Push the needle and jewelry wire through the third and final felted ball. If you added beads or other embellishments between the other two felted balls, make sure to add one here before you finish off your earrings.

16. If you want to add more length to your earrings, you can leave extra wire at the top so the felted balls will dangle lower.

17. After you have decided how long you want your earrings to be, attach the earring hook at the end. Fold the wire over and twist it back on itself so the earring hook is secured and will not slip loose.

18. Trim off any remaining wire.

19. Repeat steps 11 through 18 until you have completed your second earring.

You have now made a pair of needle felted earrings. Add this to any jewelry you previously made with felted balls, and you are well on your way to being a jewelry designer!

The basic skills that you have learned by making felted balls and using jewelry wire and earring hooks will set you on a great path to continue making more jewelry. With these patterns alone you can make matching jewelry sets of felted ball bracelets, necklaces, and now dangling earrings.

Chapter 14:

A Mouse With a Sweet Tooth

Mice are not a fan of cheese. I know, I was just as shocked as you. This myth of mice and cheese has existed for a long time, but no one really knows where it originated from. Cheese offers no nutritional value to mice. Thus, in real life, cheese should not be given to mice, particularly pet mice. Although mice will eat cheese if it is available to them (they will eat anything if it is available to them), in reality, they have more of a sweet tooth! Thankfully, this little figure is not real—even if it looks real—and can have all the cheese its little heart desires!

In these mouse instructions, there is something called a Zullitool. This is basically a wooden wand that works wonders! It has a slight butter knife shape with a rounded handle that is much smaller. You do not necessarily need to have this tool to complete this mouse figure—I have a few alternatives which I will mention below—but it is helpful. Also, this tool is great for not just one project, but you can keep it in your needle felting tool bag to use to make all sorts of shapes. The Zullitool is designed to help you make shapes quickly and consistently. To me, this sounds super helpful! It also saves your felting surface because you are making shapes on the tool versus felting onto a pad. If you are interested in purchasing one, do some Internet searches to find some available. While you are there, watch a few videos to give you a good idea of how to properly use the tool. If you do not feel like purchasing the tool, you can also use basically any skewer, pencil, or use the handle of your multi-needle tool in the same way that I am going to describe in the instructions. Just be sure to remove the needles from the tool so that you do not injure yourself! However, for this project, a pencil will probably work the best.

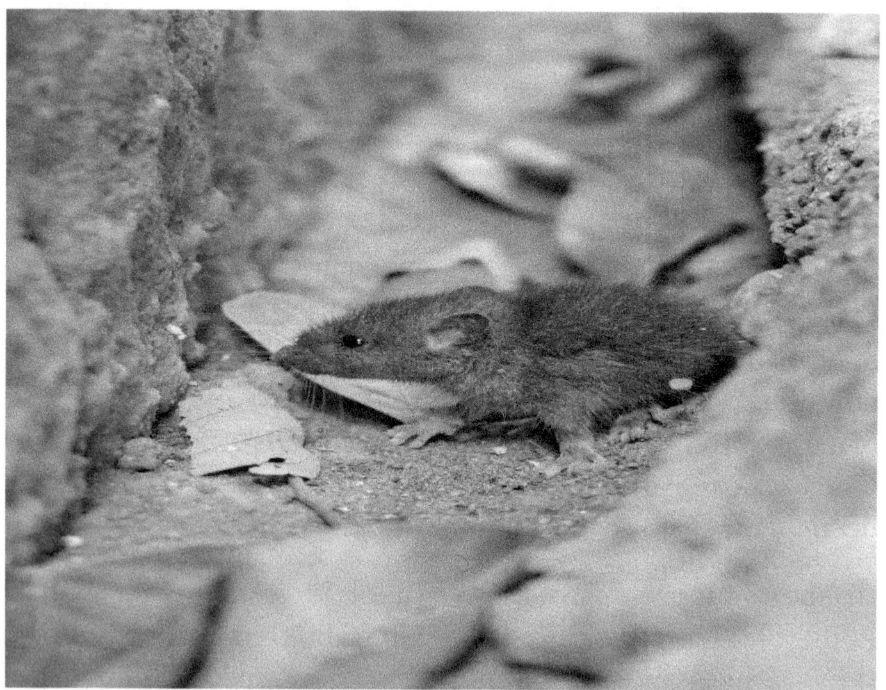

Mouse Instructions

Materials

- Zullitool
- Felting needles

- Felting wool (white, pink, and black)

- Felting pad

- Small skewer (chopstick size works)

Steps

1. Start by taking out your white or off-white wool. Section off a piece that is about 8 inches long. This first piece is going to form the core of your little mouse.

2. Take this 8 inch long piece of wool and divide it into four equal pieces along the length.

3. Take your Zullitool and begin wrapping the wool around it. Start with one corner of one of your quarter wool pieces and wrap it around the smaller end of your tool. Wrap tightly and consistently. This end of the Zullitool has a pointed end. Start wrapping just below the pointed end. Wrap two or three times, then angle the wool toward the pointed end. As you round the pointed end, angle the wool back to begin moving down the tool. Repeat this angle a couple of times. This pointed end is going to become the mouse head. By wrapping the wool repeatedly, you are creating a nice shape. Be sure to wrap tightly, holding only what wool you need to wrap once, then pulling more into the figure.

Pro-tip: When creating the head, your wool will want to slip down the tool. An easy way to avoid this is to use your non-wrapping hand to hold the wool on the tool in place. Your fingers create a sort of barrier that will help the wool stay in place.

4. You should use approximately one full quarter of wool for the head piece.

5. Take a second quarter of wool and begin forming the body. Start just below where the head stops and criss-cross your wool as you wind it around the tool. This section should take about two quarters of your wool. The head and body should be around the same size. As you criss-cross your wool, the gap between the head and body will close up. If it does not, push the body up slightly to meet the head before adding your second piece.

Pro-tip: If you are running out of wool very quickly before you get a good enough shape, chances are that you are not wrapping the wool tight enough around the tool. Never worry: this takes some practice to get used to it.

6. Take the fourth quarter of wool and begin wrapping it around the body of the mouse. Move up and cover the back of the head as well. This piece will help you join the two separate pieces together to create one tiny mouse!

7. Grab your needles and felt the wool together to make sure it is secure. Pay attention to the area where you started and ended your wool pieces.

8. Slide your wool off of the tool.

9. Take a look at the wool you just removed and decide where you want the head and body to be. There should be a natural curve already established from wrapping the wool. This is a good place to create that head and body divide.

10. When you decide where it should be, gently fold the two pieces to create a curve. Again, the wool should naturally be leaning one way over the other. Now stab it around from all directions along the neck to hold it in place. You

will know when it is ready when the head stays curled all on its own.

11. Take a strong needle (a 38 or 36 will work out well) to stab back on the bottom side of the nose to create an indent that will form the nose and mouth. This area will have a lot of give to it because it was just a simple wrap. Take your time to firm this area up. Create a fish hook style to form the mouth on the bottom side. Make sure you stay right in the center.

12. Take another 8 inch long wool and split it into four pieces. Then take one of those four pieces and cut this in half around the center so that you have two pieces approximately 4 inches long.

13. Take these two pieces and wrap them along the flat end of the Zullitool. You should be making approximately 1 inch rectangles here. Do not criss-cross when you wrap in this section. Instead, wrap the wool evenly on top of itself. You should be able to wrap the wool around at least two or three times here.

14. Slide those pieces off of the tool. Now you have two rectangular pieces that are going to become the thighs.

15. Take the rectangles one at a time and attach them to the body by felting. Let the back of the rectangle blend into the body of the mouse. The other end of the rectangle will have feet attached to them, so leave the as-is for right now.

16. Felt to keep blending the thighs onto the body and felt below to close up the bottom of the body wrap.

17. Now find your pale pink wool. Pull off a very thin strand and trim to approximately 6 inches. Make sure that the

strand is the same thickness up and down. Consistent thickness is key!

18. Find a small skewer.

19. Start about 3 inches back from the point of the skewer. Grab your pale pink wool and begin wrapping it along the skewer. Do not overlap the wool too much here: just enough to make sure there are no gaps between the wraps of your wool. If there are gaps between the wraps of the wool, the piece will not hold its shape when you slip it off of the skewers and we definitely do not want that! Again, make sure that you are pulling the wool tight and wrapping consistently up the skewer toward the pointed end.

20. Wrap the wool all the way to the pointed end, then begin to wrap backwards toward your starting point. If your wrap was not consistent, you will run out of wool. You can either stretch the remaining wool to cover what you are missing or you can begin again. It is vital that your wool stops and starts in the exact same place.

21. When you reach the starting and ending point, take the skewer between your hands and roll it vigorously. This will encourage the wool to bind to itself and keep its shape for the next step. Press firmly between the palms of your hands as you roll.

22. Slide the tail off of the skewer and pass over it with your needle a few times to make sure that it is secure.

23. Now pick up the tail from your felting pad and run it between your palms again to finish securing the wool together.

24. Take another thin strand of pale pink wool about the same 6 inches in length. Cut it in half to make two 3-inch pieces.

25. Take one of your 3-inch pieces and wrap it around the small skewer in one place. This will create a small seed shape. Do the same with the other 3-inch piece of wool.

26. Pull the seed shaped pieces off of your skewer: these will be your feet. Set them aside for a moment.

27. To make the ears, take two pieces of wool and place them on your felting pad. These pieces should be thin but not see through. Stack a few layers of wool on top of each other to create a good starting point. These pieces should look like 2-inch squares.

28. Take your needle and draw a circle that is approximately the size of a dime in the middle of these squares. This should create a circle that is bordered by loose wool.

29. Take the loose wool from the top of the circle and roll it down over the circle. Felt it into place then roll the sides into the circle, one side at a time. Felt those into place as well. All of this loose fiber should be pointing down. Leave the bottom loose and repeat for the second ear.

30. Smooth out the ears on both the front and backsides, still leaving the bottom edge loose for attachment. Check the size of the ears against your mouse head before moving on.

31. Here we are going to make a little pucker in the ear shape. Fold your ear like a taco and felt the bottom closed. Alternate from side to side to secure it properly. Here, you have the choice of how big you want to make your ear. Move the fold up or down to make the ears smaller

or larger. Once you close the pucker, you can trim off any excess wool.

32. Set the ears aside to make the very tiny nose. Stack thin layers of pink wool on top of each other to create a little quarter of an inch square.

33. Grab the tail. Felt the tail on the back of the mouse in between where the two thighs came together.

34. Grab the feet. Felt the feet one at a time onto the open fringe of the rectangular thigh that you created. Felt primarily on one end. Take a single needle and go over the other end of the foot to make sure the wrap closes up properly. It is best to start with a strong needle to secure the foot in place, then move to a finer needle to close up the wrap and smooth out the shape.

35. Now move onto the eyes. Due to the curved shape of the mouse, a closed eye looks super cute. Take a thin strand of black wool and felt a curved shape on the sides of the face.

36. Grab the ears. Find a nice space on the head behind the end of the eyes to attach the ears. There should be enough of a gap between where the eye ends and where the ear starts. Felt the loose end of the ear onto the head to secure it in place.

37. Take another thin strand of black wool to fill in the ridges of the mouth. You have already created the shape: now all you have to do is outline it!

38. Take the square for the nose and fold the sides in to create a point at the top of the shape. Try not to felt on the pad, but place the nose point side down on the mouse and felt directly on the mouse.

39. Now, you can leave the mouse this white color or you can decide to add some color to it by layering thin patches of colored wool (grey, brown, black, etc.) over top to create a nice branded top coat. If you do decide to do a color, start with the back and wrap horizontally to cover the entire body. Be sure not to cover any feet or ears!

40. Felt again to smooth out any bumps or fill in any holes.

Your mouse is now ready for a piece of cheese, or maybe not?

Pro-tip:

If ever there was a perfect figure to make even cuter, a mouse would be it. Consider changing up the overall style of this figure to make it seem more cartoonish. Add a bow or blushed cheeks. Consider making a family of mice in different shapes and sizes. Make a very plump mouse or a tiny meek mouse. This alteration can truly unlock your creativity.

You can also keep experimenting with accessories with this project. Try creating a block of cheese or give your new mice pets something sweet to nibble on: try berries or a piece of chocolate. Get creative!

Chapter 15:

Perfectly Cuddly Teddy Bear

Teddy bears are one of the most beloved stuffed creatures ever designed. Okay, perhaps that could just be my opinion; if you think about it, almost everyone has at least one teddy bear at some point in their life. Who could not want an adorable little teddy bear? Even some dogs and cats enjoy snuggling or playing with a squeaky teddy!

What I particularly love about teddy bears is that they make great gifts for people of all ages. Unlike most stuffed animals, teddy bears are given as gifts or prizes for people from young to old! How fun and lovable is that?

What is truly great about this teddy bear figure is that you can change up the size to whatever you want! Consider making a tiny figure as a quick project or a larger figure to really hone in your needle felting skills. In the instructions, I have listed brown wool as the material to use in this project. I chose the brown wool because it is a very common teddy bear color and closely resembles the color of actual bears: if you remember, one of the main goals of this book is to make realistic or semi-realistic little animals.

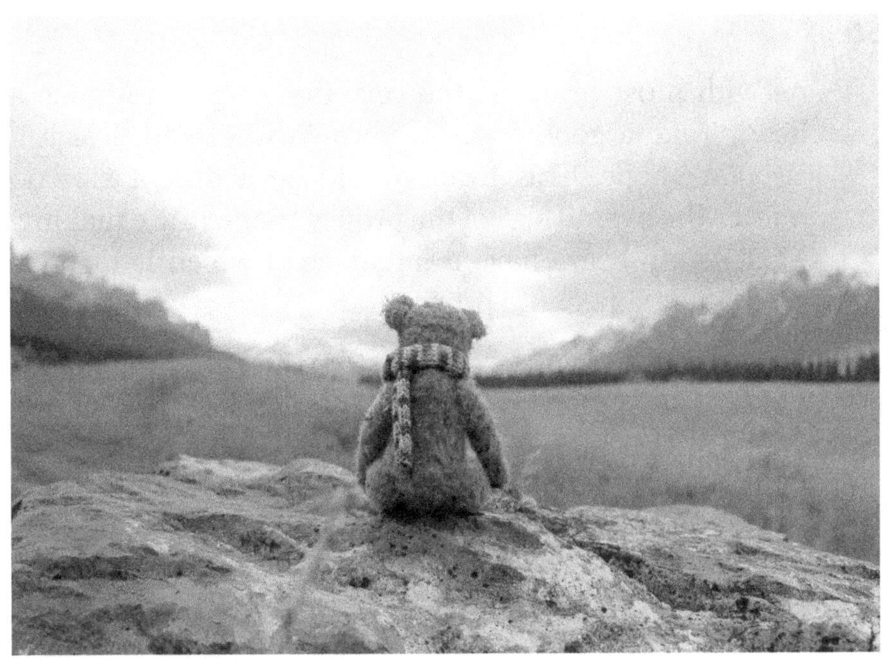

Teddy Bear Instructions

Materials

- Brown wool

- Hamanaka wool (Japanese curly wool)

- Felting needles

- Felting pad

- Plastic eyes and nose

- A red bow (size according to your bear)

- Metal wire

- Sharp scissors

Steps

1. As with most projects, the very first step is to make a head. Take a good chunk of brown wool and give it a circular shape. This head should be a decent size no matter the overall size of the project that you are making. Most teddy bears have a larger head which helps give them their super cute proportions.

2. Now take another chunk of wool and create a cylinder shaped body.

3. Next, we are going to focus on the arms and hands which will be one shape. Take a metal wire and give it a length of a hand. Twist this wire around itself to strengthen it.

4. Roll some wool around it until it becomes firm. Keep layering wool to achieve your desired level of thickness. Make sure to keep measuring it up to the body to check if the proportions work out.

5. Add some more loose wool and felt it until it is firm.

6. Create two hands of equal length and thickness. Do another proportion check before moving on.

7. To make the feet, follow the same instructions. Remember that the feet should be longer and thicker than the arms. Create a sort of mutton shape here to give dimension to the thigh and small feet. These should be one long shape.

8. Begin attaching the body parts to the torso. Start with the head. You may seal this attachment with loose wool to strengthen the figure.

9. Use some Hamanaka (Japanese wool) and felt it all around the head. Create a tight spiral starting at the top

of the head and winding down. Felt as you spiral down the figure and continue winding the curly wool past the head and onto the body. Make sure it is as even and neat as you can possibly make it.

10. Go back up to the top of the head and add more curly wool to add more dimension to the head. Be sure to blend this wool evenly. When adding wool to the top of the head you can cut small strips of the curly wool and pull it partly in your hands. Do not pull it apart too much to avoid creating holes. Only add this extra wool from the top of the head to about the middle. We will add some dimension to the face later.

11. Mark out where you want the eyes and make small cuts with your sharp scissors. After cutting the holes, poke the inside of the holes to make sure that the extra curly wool you added is firmly attached to the main head base. Attach the plastic eyes and try not to forget the glue! Wipe up any excess glue that might have leaked out.

12. Grab your normal brown wool to make the muzzle. Felt it on your pad to make it nice and firm.

13. Attach the muzzle to the face right between the eyes. Your figure will look a little funky with the two different colors at the moment. Never fear: we will be adding dimension to the face soon.

14. Now find some of the Hamanaka wool. Cut short strips of this wool and attach them to the muzzle with a thin felting needle. A thin needle is important to create a seamless and smooth layer. It is helpful to start on one side and add this extra wool across the muzzle moving from top to bottom. As you add the wool, trim the excess that might stick up or not fit with the shape of your

muzzle. It is also helpful to pull your small strips apart slightly to loosen them up and make them easy to attach smoothly. Attach the wool in sections and make sure that the muzzle is completely covered. Make sure to trim any wool that might be covering the eyes. Fill in any holes or gaps as necessary.

15. Add one last strip of extra curly wool to the center of the muzzle going from side to side.

16. Trim any excess wool to make the face neat.

17. Take some of the curly wool and make small ears. Teddy bears usually have rounded ears—make these flat. Make two of equal size and thickness.

18. Attach the ears to the top sides of your bear's head. Create a slightly curved shape when you attach the ears. Add extra layers of curly wool to strengthen the attachment and to smooth out the figure. Make sure that you add wool to all sides of the attachment. Again, use a thin felting needle for this step.

19. Grab your needle to make the curved inside of the ear more pronounced. Poke repeatedly in this area to create the desired shape.

20. Now we will attach the nose to the muzzle. In this tutorial, I have listed a plastic nose. You can attach this nose in the same way as the eyes. Cut a small hole with sharp scissors. Then, poke the inside of the hole to firm up the opening. Insert the nose with glue, then wipe up any excess glue that might have leaked out before it dries.

Pro-tip: Alternatively, you can use a polymer clay nose just like you made for Isabelle. If you have any extra noses from the Isabelle project, feel free to use them here: just make sure that the proportions line up. Do not forget to add glass varnish to make the nose nice and shiny. We would not want to see a teddy bear with a dull looking nose!

21. Grab more curly wool to add dimension to the cheeks. Use layers here and start out small. Add layers as you see fit. Use a thin felting needle to ensure a smooth addition. Follow the natural curve of the head from the mouth to the eyes. Add to your desired fluffiness and make sure both sides are of equal fluff.

Pro-tip: You can grab some acrylic paint to add some color and dimension to your teddy bear figure. Use a darker brown color to fill in the inside of the ear, around the eyes, and on the top of the nose. Alternatively, you can do this same technique with very thin pieces of darker brown wool, but this step is optional.

22. At last, take a pinch of very thin black wool and needle felt the shape of the mouth. Begin at the bottom of the plastic nose and create a natural fish hook shape along the muzzle. It is very important to use a very thin strand of black wool and to use a thin felting needle. Remember: you can add wool but you cannot take it away!

23. Now grab the hands and legs that you made earlier.

24. Take the curly wool and wrap it evenly around the shapes. Make sure that you cover well and evenly just as you did for the head and body. Cover all of the hands and legs. Make sure that the hands and legs match up appropriately.

25. Next, attach the hands to the body. Seal it and secure it using more of the curly wool. Make sure to add a layer of wool all around the attachment to fill in any gaps. Layer multiple times and felt to blend and smooth.

26. Attach the legs. This teddy bear figure is in a sitting down position: attach the legs to the side of the torso so that it can sit down properly. Attach in the same way that you just did the hands. Use layers of curly wool to seal and secure. Layer multiple times to ensure a secure attachment and felt to blend and smooth with each layer. During this step, it is also nice to extend the extra curly fur around onto the back of the body. This will help create a nice and round bottom for your teddy bear to relax on.

27. Layer more wool to fill out the inner thigh.

28. Grab some more curly wool to add more volume to the belly. We do not want any scrawny teddies here! In this stage, it is helpful to pull the curly wool apart slightly to create a really fluffy texture to felt onto your teddy bear's body.

29. Finally, tie a red bow around your teddy bear's neck to give it some adorable style! A thin ribbon of your choice works great for this final touch.

Your teddy bear is ready for cuddling!

Pro-tip:

As I mentioned before, you can make this teddy bear project any size your heart desires! Of course, tiny teddies are extremely adorable in my humble opinion. Like with other projects, an easy way to elevate this project is to make little accessories for it. We made a bow in the above tutorial that went around the teddy bear's neck. You can make a bow for the head for an easy variation, or consider making a scarf in a fun or funky color. A sweater is also a great way to add some extra cute touches to this project.

Of course, another very easy way to change up this project is to choose different colors. You can create more realistic creatures by mimicking the natural colorations of bears in the wild—think black bears, polar bears, or grizzly bears. This is a fun way to turn this project into a realistic creature.

If you are feeling that realistic styles are not quite what you are looking for in this project, consider making this teddy bear in fun and unnatural colors. The rainbow is open for any choice! Red, orange, yellow, green, blue, or violet: you decide! You can create these fun colors in a solid fur option or switch things up by creating a white belly and a colored body. This is a super cute way to make a truly dynamic little figure.

Chapter 16:

Mini Needle Felted Trees

What better project to end on than making decorative needle felted trees? Once you have the basic shape of this project done, you will have fun decorating and customizing your own trees.

This project might be last, but it is certainly not least! All of the skills you have learned up to this point will come into play with this craft. It also requires more materials than previous projects, so it is a great one to end on and leave you set up with different needles and supplies to use on future crafts. Get ready to create your miniature Christmas tree farm!

Materials Required

1. Multiple needles, needle holder, or needle felting pen

2. At least three 40 gauge felting needles, spiral or triangular

3. Beading needle and thread to match

4. Foam base

Large Christmas Tree Materials

1. Two lengths of green roving, 50 x 4 centimeters

2. One length of red roving, 25 x 2 centimeters

3. One meter of trace gold chain

4. Colorful assortment of 8 millimeter and 4 millimeter beads

This larger Christmas tree's finished size is 12 centimeters tall, with a 7 centimeter diameter at the base.

Medium Christmas Tree Materials

1. Two lengths of ivory or cream roving, 30 x 4 centimeters

2. One length of red roving, 20 x 2 centimeters

3. Twenty 4 millimeter red glass heart beads

4. One 10 millimeter red glass heart bead

This medium Christmas tree's finished size is 9 centimeters tall, with a 4.5 centimeter diameter at the base.

Small Christmas Tree Materials

1. Two lengths of green roving, 15 x 3 centimeters

2. One length of red roving, 15 x 1 centimeters

3. Forty red seed beads

This small Christmas tree's finished size is 6 centimeters tall, with a 4 centimeter diameter at the base.

Steps to Follow

For the Large Christmas Tree

1. Working on your foam mat, tease the fibers of one length of green wool roving out a little. Fold the roving over so that you have made a tall triangular shape.

2. Take the other length of green wool roving and fluff it into a ball. Insert this shape inside of the flat triangle. Make sure that you have positioned the roving so that the triangle has a fatter end that gradually tapers into a point like a carrot.

3. Pull the sides of the outer green wool roving around so that you can encase the filling.

4. Begin shaping a cone. When you are making the large Christmas tree, you can use three needles to help this step of the process go quickly.

5. Begin needle felting your layers of green wool roving together. Turn your Christmas tree as you work so that you will get a uniform roundness and texture all over the tree.

6. Cup your forefinger and thumb together to securely hold the wool in place as you shape the flat bottom. You can periodically press the bottom against a flat work surface or table to make sure you are getting it flat enough. Remember, you want these Christmas trees to be able to stand up on their own.

7. Squeeze the wool together at the top of the tree as you carefully use one needle to create a fine point. You can use a delicate needle to pull out a few fibers at a time, and continually shape them into a pointy tip with your fingers.

8. Continue felting your Christmas tree until it gets very firm. You can pause and stand your tree up on a flat surface to make sure it can stand on its own. If it starts to tilt, you can work on the bottom more to keep it even.

9. When your tree is firm and nicely formed, take thin layers of the green wool roving and layer a neat surface over the Christmas tree. This will give your tree a smooth, even finish. Start this finishing process with two needles, and as you work it to a more delicate state, you will finish with one.

10. Wrap the length of red wool (25 x 2 centimeters for the large tree, as different lengths are specified for the size of each different Christmas tree) around the bottom of the tree. Needle felt it into place to make a bright, decorative base for your tree. Tuck any spare wool underneath the tree bottom.

With this step, you can make your tree a little unique. If you do not like how far the red roving goes up on the tree, you can needle felt it to be a thinner border at the base of the tree.

11. Use straight pins to mark and measure where your decorative trimmings are going to be fixed.

12. Once you have everything mapped out, you can use loose stitches to attach the gold chain to the tree where you pinned it up.

13. Attach a special bead to the top of the tree. You can pick a slightly larger golden bead to be the centerpiece, or you can even pick a star-shaped bead. To make the bead stand tall like a tree topper, you can thread a short length of sturdy wire through the bead and down into the tip of the tree.

14. When you have positioned your beads, stitch them on with a beading needle. Add as many bead baubles necessary to make sure your Christmas tree conveys the festive spirit!

For the Medium Christmas Tree

1. Working on your foam mat, tease the fibers of one length of ivory or cream wool roving out a little. Fold the roving over so that you have made a tall triangular shape.

2. Take the other length of ivory or cream wool roving and fluff it into a ball. Insert this shape inside of the flat triangle. Make sure you have positioned the roving so that the triangle has a fatter end that gradually tapers into a point like a carrot.

3. Pull the sides of the outer ivory or cream wool roving around so that you can encase the filling.

4. Begin shaping a cone. When you are making the medium Christmas tree, you have less wool roving for the overall shape of the tree, so you will want to only use two needles. Since this is a smaller scale project, you will need to be more delicate with your needle felting process.

5. Begin needle felting your layers of ivory or cream wool roving together. Turn your Christmas tree as you work so that you will get a uniform roundness and texture all over the tree.

6. Cup your forefinger and thumb together to securely hold the wool in place as you shape the flat bottom. You can periodically press the bottom against a flat work surface or table to make sure that you are getting it flat enough. Remember, you want these Christmas trees to be able to stand up on their own.

7. Squeeze the wool together at the top of the tree as you carefully use one needle to create a fine point. You can use a delicate needle to pull out a few fibers at a time, and continually shape them into a pointy tip with your fingers.

8. Continue felting your Christmas tree until it gets very firm. You can pause and stand your tree up on a flat surface to make sure it can stand on its own. If it starts to tilt, you can work on the bottom more to keep it even.

9. When your tree is firm and nicely formed, take thin layers of the ivory or cream wool roving and layer a neat surface over the Christmas tree. This will give your tree a smooth, even finish. Start this finishing process with two needles, and as you work it to a more delicate state, you will finish with one.

10. Wrap the length of red wool (20 x 2 centimeters for this medium tree, as different lengths are specified for the size of each different Christmas tree) around the bottom of the tree. Needle felt it into place to make a bright, decorative base for your tree. Tuck any spare wool underneath the tree bottom.

With this step, you can make your tree a little unique. If you do not like how far the red roving goes up on the tree, you can needle felt it to be a thinner border at the base of the tree. You can make it look different than the larger Christmas tree, or you can make the red base look about the same across all three trees.

11. Use straight pins to mark and measure where your decorative trimmings are going to be fixed.

12. Attach the 10 millimeter glass heart bead to the top of the tree. You can thread a short length of sturdy wire through the bead and down into the tip of the tree so the bead will stand tall like a tree topper.

13. When you have positioned your red heart beads, stitch them on with a beading needle. Add as many bead baubles necessary to make sure your Christmas tree conveys the festive spirit!

For the Small Christmas Tree

1. Working on your foam mat, tease the fibers of one length of green wool roving out a little. Fold the roving over so that you have made a tall triangular shape.

2. Take the other length of green wool roving and fluff it into a ball. Insert this shape inside of the flat triangle. Make sure that you have positioned the roving so that the triangle has a fatter end that gradually tapers into a point like a carrot.

3. Pull the sides of the outer green wool roving around so that you can encase the filling.

4. Begin shaping a cone. When you are making the large Christmas tree, you can use three needles to help this step of the process go quickly.

5. Begin needle felting your layers of green wool roving together. Turn your Christmas tree as you work so that you will get a uniform roundness and texture all over the tree.

6. Cup your forefinger and thumb together to securely hold the wool in place as you shape the flat bottom. You can periodically press the bottom against a flat work surface or table to make sure you are getting it flat enough. Remember, you want these Christmas trees to be able to stand up on their own.

7. Squeeze the wool together at the top of the tree as you carefully use one needle to create a fine point. You can use a delicate needle to pull out a few fibers at a time, and continually shape them into a pointy tip with your fingers.

8. Continue felting your Christmas tree until it gets very firm. You can pause and stand your tree up on a flat surface to make sure it can stand on its own. If it starts to tilt, you can work on the bottom more to keep it even.

9. When your tree is firm and nicely formed, take thin layers of the green wool roving and layer a neat surface over the Christmas tree. This will give your tree a smooth, even finish. Start this finishing process with two needles, and as you work it to a more delicate state, you will finish with one.

10. Wrap the length of red wool (15 x 1 centimeters for the small tree, as different lengths are specified for the size of each different Christmas tree) around the bottom of the tree. Needle felt it into place to make a bright, decorative base for your tree. Tuck any spare wool underneath the tree bottom.

With this step, you can make your tree a little unique. If you do not like how far the red roving goes up on the tree, you can needle felt it so that you have a thinner border at the base of the tree. You can make it look different than the large and medium Christmas trees, or you can make the red base look about the same on all three trees.

11. Use straight pins to mark and measure where your decorative trimmings are going to be fixed.

12. Attach a special bead to the top of the tree. You can pick a slightly larger bead to be the centerpiece, or you can even pick a star-shaped bead. To make the bead stand tall like a tree

topper, you can thread a short length of sturdy wire through the bead and down into the tip of the tree.

13. When you have positioned your red seed beads beads, stitch them on with a beading needle. Add as many bead baubles necessary to make sure your Christmas tree conveys the festive spirit!

Your needle felted trees are ready! This trio of trees will make an adorable centerpiece for your holiday meals. If you do not have room on the table, consider putting them on the mantel or a side table so all of your guests can "ooh" and "ahh" over the cuteness as they enter your winter wonderland.

Conclusion

Now that you have learned the basics of needle felting, you will be well on your way to developing your own patterns and products.

Needle felting is a therapeutic craft, mostly due to the repetitive motions of working the needle into the fibers. It has recently grown in popularity, rivaling the coloring book trend of a few years ago.

Needle felting is a great task you can do to destress. You can work the fibers into felt while watching a TV show or movie, and working them into a sculpture only takes a little more focus.

To get ideas on needle felting crafts you can make, just look around! Have you been wanting some new decorations for your house? Now you can needle felt your own! Make ornaments or garland like those you have learned while working through this book. Use needle felt writing to create a beautiful quote to hang on your wall. You added needle felt writing onto a pillowcase in Chapter 8, which you can definitely do again, but why not try your hand at needle felting an entire pillow? You can even needle felt a cute little set of teacups to display in your kitchen!

Think about the kind of jewelry you like to wear, or what you would give as gifts. If any of your friends wear dangly earrings, you can use the felted ball earrings pattern from this book to make pairs for them. You can also use the felted balls to make bracelets and statement necklaces.

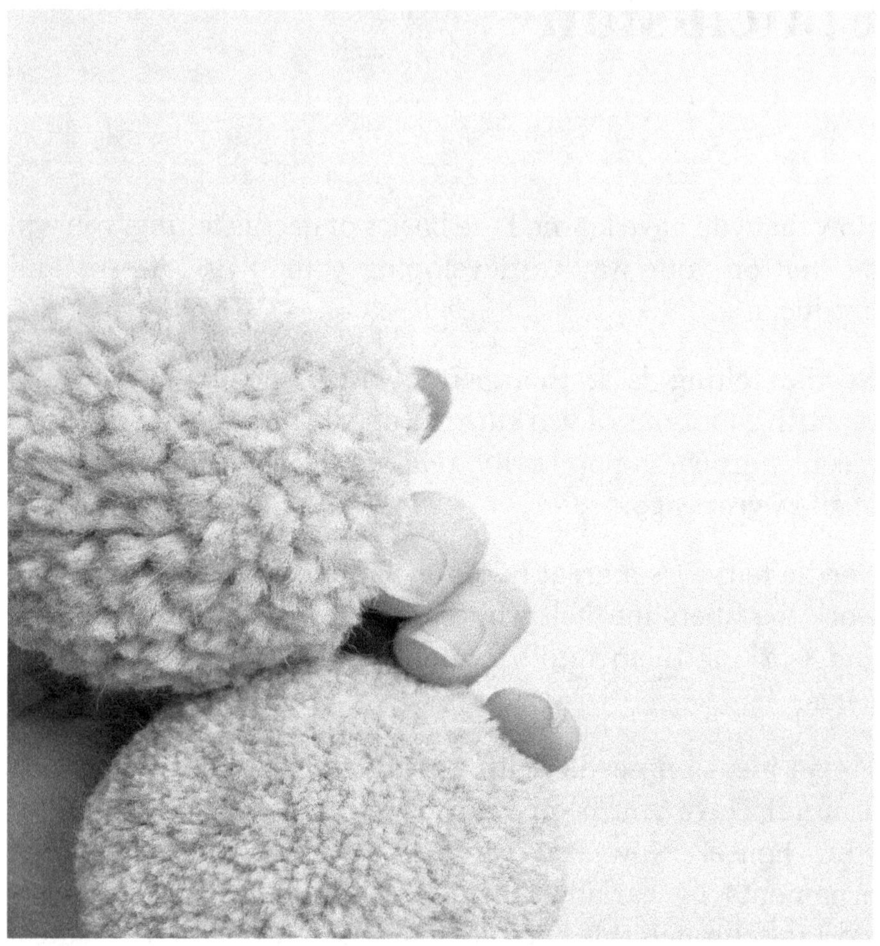

The needle felted cherry bag charms is also a great jumping off point to make more needle felted fruits. You can make the fruits miniature so they can dangle from key rings, or you can make them bigger—or even to scale!—and display them as decorative sculptures. If you like the idea of key rings and bag charms, you are not limited to fruits—you can design colorful balls, or go back to the first project you ever did and make flat needle felted shapes to hang from key rings.

Everyone loves adorable needle felted animals, and you learned how to make a few in this book. If you want to try making other needle felted animals, think of your favorite critters. Do you love your puppy or kitty more than anything in the world? Try to make a needle felted version of them. You can make needle felted versions of family pets for your friends as well, or even open yourself up for commissions.

If you are interested in taking commissions, selling your own products, or even if you just want to see what other people are making, Etsy is the place to go. Many fiber artists are selling their wares on Etsy, so it is a great place to find inspiration. If you need patterns, a lot of artists sell them. You can also look around at various crafters' and fiber artists' blogs for inspiration and free tutorials.

Tips to Take Away

After doing the projects in this book, you are well on your way to being an advanced needle felter! For quick reference, here are the top five tips to remember as you continue your crafting work.

1. Keep Your Needle Straight

Whether you are using a standard notched needle, triangle needle, star needle, twisted needle, or reverse needle, you will want to keep it straight. Whatever angle you insert the needle into the wool fibers, you need to pull it back out in that same way. If you poke the needle into the fibers and try to pull it out as hard as you can, you might break off the tip of your needle.

You also want to keep your needle straight while it is in the fibers. If you bend it slightly, it could break due to the tangles gripping the notches of the needle. For this reason, it is best to use a consistent up and down motion when needle felting.

2. Do Not Force It

If you try to insert the needle into your fibers and are not able to, do not keep pushing! It might break the tip of your needle. Being unable to poke your needle into a certain area of fibers might mean that the section is already completely felted. In that case, you can move on to another section. If you think the resistant area still needs more agitation, then you can use a needle with a smaller gauge to finish the delicate work.

3. Work Evenly

Moving the fibers around as you felt will keep your work even. You want to make sure that all areas are equally stiff so your final project will look cohesive and sturdy. Use your fingers to feel the texture of the fibers as you needle felt, but make sure you are always aware of where your fingers are in relation to your needles. You do not want to poke yourself with one of these notched needles!

4. Felt in Layers

Instead of starting with a large chunk of wool fibers and working hard to felt it all, start with smaller amounts. As you felt a small portion of wool, you can layer more raw fiber on top and work it into what you have already completed. Adding fibers in later will not be a problem if you remember to work evenly and rely on the wool's overall texture to let you know when all fibers are consistent.

5. Use a Base

Instead of using short fiber wool as a core for all of your projects, you can use foam or wire to form a base. Think about this step as you are planning your pattern so that you can save on wool. Using wire to form an animal's body will not only save your money and wool, but it will also cut down on the steps needed to complete the project.

If you are making stuffed animals instead of sculptures, you can use pillow stuffing at the center of your project to keep it cuddly. If you need something firmer but still soft, you can try quilt batting. The options are limitless, so use your imagination!

References

13 needle felting projects for beginners. (n.d.). Gathered. Retrieved November 5, 2020,
from
https://www.gathered.how/arts-crafts/13-needle-felting-projects-for-beginners/

Alexas_Fotos. (2016). Flower Felt Orange Greeting. In *Pixabay*.
https://pixabay.com/photos/flower-felt-orange-greeting-card-1593467/

Alicja. (2019). Felt Scroll Material. In *Pixabay*.
https://pixabay.com/photos/felt-scroll-material-web-colorful-4007361/

Ariyo, S. (2019). black lokai photo. In *Unsplash*.
https://unsplash.com/photos/zlROZagixXY

Art, S. F. (2017, February 16). *Sarafina Fiber Art: Using Wire in Needle Felting*.
Sarafina Fiber Art.
http://sarafinafiberartblog.blogspot.com/2017/02/using-wire-in-needle-felting.
html

dreamwalker9. (2016b). Teddy Bear Needle Felting. In *Pixabay*.
https://pixabay.com/photos/teddy-bear-needle-felting-toy-1767729/

Eleanor Stanwood. (2014, June 23). Martha's Vineyard Arts & Ideas.

    http://www.mvartsandideas.com/2014/06/eleanor-stanwood/

Håland, J. (2018). two white sheep photo. In *Unsplash*.
    https://unsplash.com/photos/jPZvbjknC4E

Hermann, S., & Richter, F. (2017). Marguerite Heart Wood. In *Pixabay*.

    https://pixabay.com/photos/marguerite-heart-wood-ivy-blossom-2380664/

HeungSoon. (2018a). Leather Craft Needle Thread. In *Pixabay*.

    https://pixabay.com/photos/leather-craft-needle-thread-sew-3556442/

How Needle Felting Began—Felting Fridays. (n.d.). Star Magnolias. Retrieved

    November 9, 2020, from
    https://starmagnolias.com/blogmain/2016/11/18/how-needle-felting-began-felti
    ng-fridays

How to needle felt. (n.d.). WikiHow. Retrieved November 5, 2020, from
    https://www.wikihow.com/Needle-Felt

How To Use Wire For Needle Felting—Plus Mini Tutorial. (n.d.).

    Lincolnshirefenncraftsblog.com. Retrieved November 9, 2020, from
    https://lincolnshirefenncraftsblog.com/2020/04/17/how-to-use-wire-for-needle
    -felting-plus-mini-tutorial/

Schrøder, N. (2018). person holding white fur textile photo. In *Unsplash*.
        https://unsplash.com/photos/z2CnusvHDco

Stux. (2014). Sheep's Wool Sheep Wool-Felt. In *Pixabay*.
        https://pixabay.com/photos/sheep-s-wool-sheep-wool-felt-533756/

Stux. (2018). Felt Balls Sheep's Wool Natural. In *Pixabay*.
        https://pixabay.com/photos/felt-balls-sheep-s-wool-3319208/

INTERMEDIATE GUIDE
TO
NEEDLE FELTING

ARI YOSHINOBU

Time to Get Ready

Congrats on your completion of the beginner's guide, and welcome to the very first stages of completing your intermediate guide! It makes me so happy to see you here with me again. We have come a long way together, and I hope you are as excited to jump into this new guide as much as I am!

One of the best parts about learning needle felting is that there is never a shortage of things to learn. This is what I love most about this skill and art form; yes, before you ask, it is an art form. I hope that you view your work as art too. A lot of hard work and technical skill goes into making each little creature or figure; those ideas are the very foundation of what art means. There is a lot of destruction in the world: to make something and put it forth into the world is truly special. I hope that you see how much good creative expression does for you and for everyone else around you.

Before we jump into new material, how about we take a moment to review what we learned in the beginner's guide. Since we covered so much in the first guide, it is good to take this moment to refresh what you know before we jump into new projects.

In the beginner's guide, we learned what needle felting is and how the basic principle is relatively simple. All you need to complete a basic structure is a piece of wool and a barbed needle. However, we do not want to stick to making basic structures all the time, do we?

After that, we jumped into the necessary tools needed to complete a felted figure. We mentioned wool and a barbed needle already; the last tool needed is a surface to felt on.

Now, let us test your memory. There are four different types of felting needles: can you name them? Try your best to name them here, and I will include the answers at the end of this section. No peeking!

We also reviewed the different types of wool available. What is your favorite wool that you have used so far? Which wool are you most excited to try out? I love how each wool lends a different texture and feel to each new project. Even if you make the same shape over and over again, using different yarns will result in different products. How fun is that?

Finally, we jumped into some super cute projects together. What was your favorite project that we completed together? Are there any projects that you skipped over? If so, I greatly encourage you to go back and try whichever task you skipped. Did you struggle with any projects or techniques in a task? Again, I strongly encourage you to go back and try them again. As I'm sure you know, practice makes perfect. Each of the projects listed in the beginner's guide are made to teach you vital skills that will help you improve your needle felting projects. By going back and trying difficult techniques or structures multiple times, you are building a stronger understanding and will help you build a stronger technique. Naturally, and over time, you will get better and your hard work will pay off; that is the whole reason you are here in this intermediate guide, right?

Now that we have reviewed the information we learned in the beginner's guide, let us now get to learning new skills! In this guide, we will learn how to make some advanced shapes and work toward making realistic figures. Here, we are going to focus on super cute animal projects with a few that we can alter to reach peak cuteness!

As in the beginner's guide, each of these projects were carefully selected to help you improve your skills. These projects build on the foundation that you formed in the beginner's guide and introduce you to new techniques, new wool fibers, and even a few new tools! I have also included a hand section of tips, tricks, and advice for you to check out. Keep this section close by as I will make references to it during the individual projects. These tips, tricks, and advice are not 'one size fits all': these are things that work great for some people but may not work the best for everyone. I encourage you to at least try them out and modify the suggestions in a way that feels natural to you.

If your goal is to focus on more realistic figures, I included photos of the real animals in natural colors and settings to give you an immediate reference. This will save you the trouble of having to do an Internet search to see what an ermine looks like and then fall into an Internet hole after you discover how cute their little faces are and completely ignore your needle felting project. We do not want this, so I made it simple for you to help you along your journey.

If you are still feeling a little weak on your feet in regard to your needle felting ability, I encourage you to start out by making the projects as they are written. Having that step-by-step instruction to keep flipping back to will help you gain confidence in your abilities. Once you feel more confident, try out some of the tips and tricks in the projects, or alter the instructions slightly to create a figure that is truly your own.

That being said, there are opportunities to take all of these projects a step further. At the end of each project, I list some ideas of how you can modify the figures to create different and related creatures. These are just suggestions—you by no means have to follow them. They are there just to spark your creativity and encourage you to think about projects in different ways. I hope you like the ideas, and I hope they help you think of other ways that you can use these projects to create even more projects! If you think of ideas, feel free to jot them down so that you do not forget them later on.

Most importantly, as you start to dive into these projects, take your time going through them. Learning how to needle felt is a marathon, not a sprint. If you rush through all of the projects, you are going to make mistakes and break a few needles, which will lead to frustration. Rushing is not necessary, and frustration is certainly not ideal. Slow and steady practice is much more relaxing and enjoyable! Take your time and enjoy making nine new little creatures!

Take a moment right now to flip back to the table of contents. Check out the projects that are available to you in this book. What are you most excited to make? Are there any projects that you are hesitant about? Do your best to try out each project at least once: I guarantee that you will learn something new and have lots of fun doing it.

Let us raise our needles to the beginning of your new journey to becoming a pro in needle felting—just watch out for that pointy end! We would not want any injuries before you start creating any projects.

*Four types of needles: triangle, star, twisted/spiral, and reverse. Did you get any of them? All four? Look at you go, you rockstar!

Chapter 1:

Needle Felting Tips and Tricks

Needle felting is an art that should be truly admired. It takes great patience and hard work to make the beautiful figures that you see all across the Internet. Thankfully, the art of needle felting has grown in popularity in the past few years. This is good news for beginners or ones at the intermediate level because you have so many tools and tricks literally at your fingertips. In the beginner's guide, you learned a lot of important skills and information, but there is always room for improvement. Collecting advice—like in this next section and on the Internet in guides and tutorials—will help you keep reaching and achieving your goals. Seeking out this information will also help motivate you to reach for higher goals as you grow. I hope that these nine little projects make your fingers itch with creative energy and encourage you to seek new projects beyond what is in this guide. With so many adorable projects out there, who would not want to try to get better?

As we discussed before, there is always something new to learn during your needle felting journey. In this chapter, I have compiled a group of tips and tricks to help your journey from beginner to expert go smoothly. Some of these are best practices that will help you successfully master a skill; others are suggestions that people have found to work well for them. Take each tip as a tip. You by no means have to follow any of these ideas. All I ask of you is that you take a few moments to try out the suggestions when you are completing projects. If you never try them, how will you know if you like them or not?

No matter what, I hope you come away from this chapter with new knowledge and armed with techniques that will help you reach the next level in your needle felting journey.

Time to dig in!

Tips, Tricks, and Advice

Before Felting

1. When you have a small piece of wool, before starting, rub the wool between your hands. This will help to bring the individual fibers together and help you get a head start on your felting.

2. When you have medium or large sheets of wool, keep them in their sheet formation. This saves you the headache—and extra work—of smoothing out unnecessary bumps later on. Trust me: you will thank me for this tip later.

3. It is always best to start small: with wool, that is. If you are unsure of the amount of wool that you may need to start a project, start off with a small amount, then add as needed. You can always add wool to a project, but you cannot take it away; you would not want your elephant head turning into a rock hard boulder, would you?

4. When a project calls for a large, round piece, you can save on wool and time by starting with balls of acrylic or polyfill. You can either gather the acrylic together and begin felting it into a sphere, then cover it in wool or take polyfill and wrap thin yarn or thread all around it to create a dense ball, covering with wool once again. This is a great way to save money on wool and cut corners in a larger project that will not disrupt the end result of your project.

5. In a similar suggestion, when creating larger round shapes, you can start by tying a knot or two in the center of your shape: this will help you form a firm core and help you complete a round shape faster.

6. Your needles are going to break: it is inevitable. Felting needles are naturally fragile. It is an excellent practice to keep extra needles nearby when you are starting or working on a project. That way, when one inevitably breaks, you can pick up a new needle and keep going. You do not want anything disrupting your flow once you find it!

7. It is a good habit when starting a project—particularly if it comes in a kit with a limited wool supply—to set aside a little bit of each type or color of wool. This way, when you have completed the project, you can use the wool that you set aside to fix any imperfections or mistakes.

8. If you can, invest in some stencils or cookie cutters to use as guides for small projects. This only works for small flat shapes but greatly helps you form and shape your desired piece. Take your cookie cutter or stencil and stuff it with wool, then begin poking. Keep the wool within the stencil and flip it over to begin poking the other side. Do this poke, flip, poke dance until the wool becomes firm

and is in the shape that you desire. When the wool has taken shape, focus on cleaning up the edges. Only remove the stencil or cutter when you are confident that the wool will hold its shape.

9. No one wants sore fingers: get in the good habit of holding your wool so that you can see your fingers at all times. Move slowly and carefully when you begin to poke to avoid hitting your fingers.

During Felting

1. Patience is key when starting a new project. When you pick up a new piece of wool, it can be hard to see how a soft and fluffy piece can turn into a dense shape of your desire. Be patient and begin to poke. Only after approximately 5-10 minutes will you start to see the wool firm up. The more you poke, the more the fibers will get tangled up together and the smaller your wool will become. It is important not to rush this stage. Take your time when forming your shapes. Rushing to get soft wool to become dense will just result in broken needles and broken spirits. Think of it like a smooth rhythm.

2. Consider investing in a needle felting pen. A needle felting pen allows you to use multiple needles at one time versus a single needle. Naturally, this does speed up your process dramatically. Of course, this is not a necessary investment but it will save you time. There are many styles available at your local and online craft stores. I encourage you to check them out even just to see how they work. Consider watching a few videos first to see if this tool is something you are interested in.

3. Pull the needle out in the same direction that you put it in. This is perhaps the most important tip of all, so it bears repeating. Pull the needle out in the exact same direction that you intend to put it in! It is not about pressure, but straight/precise angles. When you push a needle in and bring it out at a different angle, you will most likely break the needle. Not only is this a headache because it stalls your progress, when you unnecessarily break a needle it can be dangerous. You can poke yourself or lose half of the needle for someone else to poke themselves later on. If you do break a needle, as everyone eventually does, be sure to keep track of the pieces and promptly remove or dispose of them to save yourself from injury.

4. Do not force the needle into the wool. Again, needle felting is not about pressure but precise and straight angles. You will break your needles if you force it into the wool. As shapes become denser, move slower. This will not only help you stay uniform, it will also help you avoid breaking needles.

5. What do you do if you break a needle? Think of this as a large splinter. Gently squeeze the wool to expose the broken needle inside your shape. Be careful not to put your fingers in the spot where the needle is. Find some tweezers and carefully, yet firmly remove the needle from the shape. Try not to pull it at a wrong angle, just like when you are working. Another option to remove a broken needle from inside a wool piece is to find scissors and make small cuts around the area where the needle disappeared. Remember when we were smart and saved little pieces of wool before we started our project? This is the perfect time to break out a piece to patch up the hole

that you just cut into your project. Felt the loose pieces of wool into the hole to close it up.

6. For round objects, uniformity is key. Do not poke in one place repeatedly. Instead, move around your shape in a uniform way and poke randomly but evenly. When creating round objects, you should move the figure with almost every poke to ensure that you are poking all around. If you do not move the sphere around and only poke in one area, you will not be creating a round sphere, but you will be creating unwanted dimples and shapes. Think about it: if with every poke the wool gets denser and smaller, then poking in one area 10 times but in another area only two times will result in a lopsided sphere.

7. Small pieces can be difficult to attach to larger pieces. A pro tip is to leave some loose wool on your pieces at the exact place that you will later attach the pieces together. Visualize cotton candy here. You will have a dense shape with wispy or fluffy pieces on the ends. A further pro tip: try not to eat the wool. Unfortunately, it is not actually cotton candy. Anyone hungry for some sugar right now?

8. In some projects, you may desire to use plastic pieces for eyes or noses. A great tip is to mark the spot where you want to attach the plastic piece with a needle. Then, find your trusty scissors and make a small cut in that exact area. Find some glue and add it to your plastic piece. Promptly insert the plastic piece into the hole. I like to hold the piece for a few seconds to make sure the glue gets all up in the wool before it dries.

9. If you find yourself adding a new and fluffy piece of wool onto an almost completed shape—maybe you are filling

a hole from a broken needle or you are adding wool to make the shape bigger—do not poke too hard. If you do, your shape will become distorted; no one wants a distorted wolf body, do we?

10. You will know when a shape is almost complete when the piece begins to firm up and become difficult to poke. When you get to this point, do a little happy dance to celebrate your new shape!

Finishing Up

1. If you complete your shape only to find little gaps left in your final project, you can try rolling small balls of wool between your fingers. Insert and put felt on these small balls into the gaps in your shape to fill them up.

2. If you complete your shape and find that you are not happy with the end result, feel free to lift up the wool with your needle (gently, of course). Only pick up the top layers of wool here. Add some of the extra wool that you smartly set aside at the beginning of the project to fill in the gaps that you just created and redo the shape or redo the details that you are unhappy with.

3. If you are making small details with wool—particularly in faces—be sure not to use too much wool at the beginning. This is an area that people often start with way too much and then have bulky features. If you do this, it is okay. Chalk it up to a learning experience and remember to use less next time. Like we have said before, it is easier to add wool to enhance features than it is to remove wool.

Tools

When you are just starting out, you do not need a ton of equipment to make figures. However, there are some tools and accessories that can make needle felting easier or even help make your techniques neater and better. Here are some tools that are not necessary but that you might want to invest in at some point in your needle felting journey.

1. Needle felting needles. If you are here, chances are you already have one or two needles. As you continue to learn, it is good to start building up your needle collection. Invest in getting different sized needles and back up needles for when your main needles inevitably break. They are going to break: a lot. Even when you are an expert. Felting needles come in many sizes from strong to thin. Each needle has a different effect and will produce a different end result. It is recommended that you have at least a strong and thin needle to do both binding and detail work. As you can assume, a strong needle is harsher and helps you firm up the shapes that you want to make. Whereas the thin needle helps you smooth out the shapes that you have made and add small delicate details, like facial features.

2. Needle felting pen. This tool allows you to hold multiple needles at the same time. This helps you create shapes in almost half the time of a single needle. Just think about it: instead of one single needle poking in one area at a time, a pen allows you to make multiple pokes in multiple areas at the same time. Sounds pretty great, right? Do some Internet searches or check out your local craft store to find what is available to you. These are typically not very expensive, and in my opinion, a good tool to add to your belt.

3. Felting thimbles. Yes! Felting thimbles exist. I am sure by now you have poked yourself at least once or twice. If you have, you know how terribly painful this can be. Felting needles help you protect your precious fingers. I mean, how can you create figures if your fingers are too sore? Felting thimbles do not seem to be too popular in the mainstream felting community. Where I have noticed people who use them absolutely love them. The ones I have seen have been made out of a thick leather which protects your fingers in a stylish way! The thick leather is great, because it is extremely difficult to puncture at the pressure level that you should be needle felting. Remember, pressure is not important when felting but instead accurate and straight pokes.

4. Sharp scissors. Most people have at least one set of scissors in their house already, but chances are, these scissors are multi-functional. If you use your household scissors to cut everything under the sun, chances are they might be kind of dull. Think about investing in a sharp pair that is just for your needle felting figures. If you do this, look for a small pair with sharp ends. This will help you make precise cuts like with eye and nose attachments.

5. Felting mat. Chances are that you already have some version of this tool, but there are lots of types of mats out there! Do some research to see what types are available to you and consider trying out a few. There are bristled mats, common foam mats, sponge foam mats, or homemade pin cushion type mats. Be like Goldilocks and figure out which type of mat is just okay and which type of mat is just right for you.

6. Zullitool. In some of the projects in this guide, the materials list calls for what is called a Zullitool. This is a cool new tool that is super helpful to make a variety of shapes. The tool itself looks almost like a wooden wand, which is a fitting description for something that is so magical. This tool has two sides: a flat one inch side and a small skewer on the other side. Both of these ends are used to wrap wool around to create body shapes versus felting a flat piece of wool into a 3-D shape. This is great for smaller projects and it helps you save wool. Later in the mouse tutorial, we will put this tool to use. I will also talk about alternatives that you can use if you do not want to buy a Zullitool right off the bat. These alternatives are a great way to try out a similar technique and see if you like it.

Like I said, you do not need a lot of tools to complete even complicated figures. This is good news if you do not wish to buy a lot of extra tools or would not want to spend the extra money. Of course, I am not suggesting or expecting you to go out and buy these tools all in one go. If you do want to purchase some, consider buying only what you need when you need it or per new project. This is a cost effective way to add versatile tools to your toolbelt without breaking the bank.

Important Advice to Remember

1. Practice, practice, practice. The only way you are going to get better at needle felting is to practice. When you are learning, it is good to set aside time every week to work on a project. Now, I am not asking you to set aside 30 hours a week to pure needle felting practice: we need to be realistic. However, when you set time aside every week to intentionally practice felting, you are committing to learning the practice. Every minute that

you put into this skill will pay off down the line. Before you know it, you will be a needle felting rockstar!

2. When you get into a practice rhythm, create a little ritual around your practice. You have already carved out this time, now use it as a moment of self-care. Put on your favorite album, show, or movie. Pour yourself a cup of your favorite hot drink—pro tip: hot chocolate and needle felting go hand in hand—or even burn a new candle. Whatever you enjoy or whatever relaxes you, combine it with your needle felting practice. This will help you create a relaxing flow; if you get frustrated at a technique or structure, then you can pause for a moment, take a few deep breaths, or a few sips of your hot drink and reset. Use this moment to take stock of what you are doing and what is making you frustrated and fix it.

3. Finally, and perhaps most importantly, never compare yourself to other needle felting artists. I know that it is instinct to see examples of experts doing incredible things with wool and you think to yourself that you will never be able to do that. Trust in the practice, trust in the time and effort that you put in, and trust in yourself. You are not going to be an expert right away. Everyone finds their own groove in their own time. Let yourself get there because you will with time and practice. Everyone started out as a beginner/novice just like you, too. Remember, every "imperfection" is not an "imperfection" but what makes the figure uniquely yours. You can have a group of a hundred people follow the same instructions, and guaranteed, every single figure will look differently. This is what makes the art of needle felting! Take ownership of your figures, even your very first ones. Just try not to get all Dr. Frankenstein on me!

Final Thoughts on Tips, Tricks, and Advice

What tips and tricks did you enjoy the most? Have you discovered any of these in one of your beginner-style projects? Which tip or trick are you most excited to employ in your next needle felting project?

As you will come to find out, what works for one person may not work for another. Keep an open mind when you approach projects, and try out new things until you figure out just what works for you. I also encourage you to find other people that are interested in needle felting. Finding a person or a community is a great way to expand your knowledge, work on your skills, and meet some pretty cool people along the way! You can start by checking out blogs or videos on the Internet. With an expanding interest in needle felting in the craft world, felting blogs are growing, too. Do some quick searches and see what is out there. If you do not feel comfortable jumping into conversations, then just take a back seat and see what other people in this community are doing. As you get to know what is out there, start adding comments to various projects. Ask questions about something that you are unsure of, and be sure to tell them how much you enjoyed their material. Everyone needs some positivity and encouragement in their lives; be a source of light!

Now, who is ready to dive into their next needle felting project?

Chapter 2:

Wandering Wolf

Both feared and revered, wolves have been a part of human history and storytelling for as long as people have been around. In western culture, the story of Little Red Riding Hood probably comes to mind first or maybe even the story of the Three Little Pigs. If you are a fan of wolves, you might find these stories to be degrading toward wolves. If you are fearful of wolves, then maybe you think that these stories are just right. Whatever you think, these stories showcase one important trait about wolves: how smart and foreboding they can be.

These stories were created out of sheer human instinct for survival. Wolves were notorious for preying on and killing livestock that were vital to feeding the human population. So, if wolves were the bad guys in stories, then they became the bad guys in real life and their removal would not seem like such a bad idea. This idea reigns supreme in communities that relied on farming to survive. In communities that relied on hunting, the image of a wolf was entirely different. It is no wonder human communities that relied on hunting would admire and even attempt to mimic wolf hunting patterns.

Nowadays, wolves rarely come in contact with most humans. This is mainly out of this century and the long fear of being hunted by humans. In most areas, the wolf population is relatively low—especially compared to the human population—which means that wolves and humans live entirely separate from each other. This is good for wolves and humans alike but perhaps not so good for human storytelling; however, that is still okay: humans have never run out of bad guys to put in their stories.

The gray wolf is the largest and most common of the wolf species. From this, there are a handful of subspecies that exist (think coyotes, dingoes, jackals, hyenas, and even the domestic dog). These subspecies are so closely related that hybrid species are possible, although dangerous if domesticated.

Wolves also live in strong communities on which they depend upon for food and survival. If you have a few minutes, check out some videos of wolves hunting. Their strategy is incredible and very captivating to watch!

The fur of a wolf is typically mottled and common colors include white, brown, gray, and black. Although wolves appear to be mostly one color, it is a combination of these four colors that make up the appearance of a single solid coloration. This effect makes this project extremely unique. If you are looking for a more streamlined project the first time around, you can make an all white, brown, or black wolf because they do exist in nature. If you are looking to try out some new skills, I encourage you to try at least a mix of two colors to make up the wolf's fur or even try all three if you are very adventurous.

Do not forget that the ears and muzzle of a wolf have a slightly pointed style and the tail is nice and fluffy.

There is nothing to fear about this first project. In fact, this little figure is far more adorable and playful than menacing and definitely deserves a spot on your shelf next to your other projects. Now, all you have to do is get to making this little guy or gal!

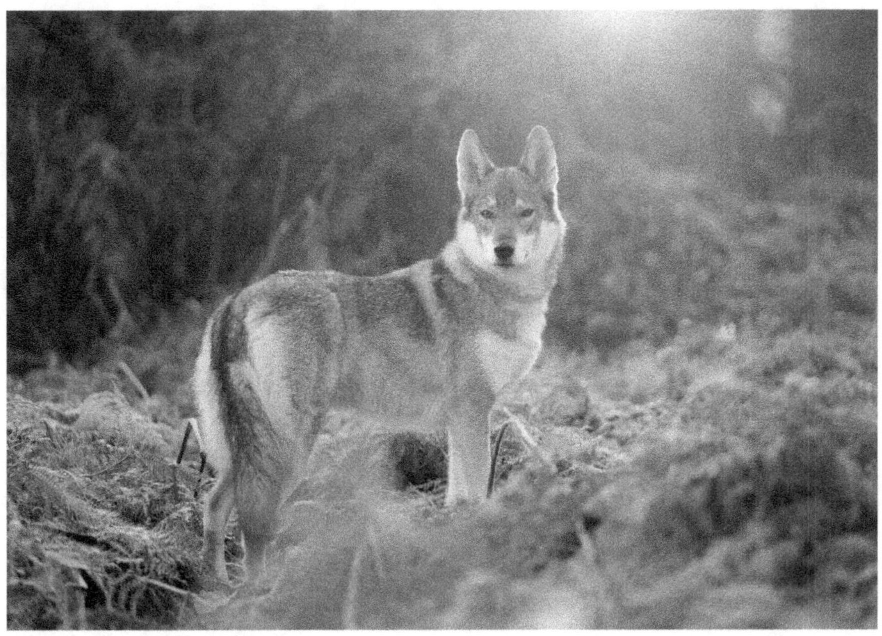

Wolf Instructions

Materials

- Metal wife for skeleton

- Felting needles

- Felting pad

- Wolf spunk

- Black, natural color, and brown roving

Steps

1. Grab your metal wire. For this step, you can either cut the wire to the size that you would like or you can leave it attached and cut it after you have created your wire skeleton.

2. Make a rough skeleton of the wolf with the wire. Start with the head by adding a slight bend to the wire. Bend the wire again to create the distinction between the neck and the body. From here, mark out the length that you want your back to be and snip off the wire. Twist extra wire evenly on top of the head, neck, and back end to create a stronger structure. Add wire in a v-shape to the front and back to create the legs. Make sure to wrap these wires together to strengthen again. Finally, add some curves to the legs (particularly in the hind legs because they have the most natural curve), including bends for the feet here as well. Add wire to any section that feels particularly weak. Think about the head, neck, and legs that are going to hold the most weight.

3. Take natural color felt and wrap tightly around the skeleton to form a base. We wrap a layer tightly at first to build a good base that we can next felt onto it to keep building up the body.

4. Add more layers to keep building up the body. By this point, you should be able to needle felt to tighten the wool and hold it in place.

5. Now, start slowly adding layers on it to give it a proper mass.

6. Add detail figures to it like paws, a tail, etc.

7. After that, use black felt to make eyes and a nose on the face of the wolf.

8. Mix some natural color and brown felt together to create that fun branded, or varied, fur that is very common in wolves.

9. Add it on the sculpture to add details of the wolf.

10. Now, needle felt the ears of the wolf using the same mixed felt. Make sure to create a slightly curved shape to the ears. You cannot send you wolf out into the world not being able to hear properly!

11. Add more details to the body of the wolf with the help of the wolf spunk.

12. Add details to the tail and use multiple needles for better results. The multiple needles with help create a fluffy tail. Follow the natural curve of a wolf's tail by adding fluff as it gets farther away from the body then coming to almost a point at the end.

13. At last, take some black felt and add details to the paw and needed areas.

Now your wolf is ready to hunt.

Pro-tip:

Want to take this project a step further and truly unlock your felting skills? Consider using this shape to create some of the subspecies of the gray wolf. Do some image research to find examples of coyotes, dingoes, and different types of wolves based on location like the Italian wolf, Indian plains wolf, red wolf, etc. Alter the size and slight shape based on the new species of your choice. This is also a fun way to experiment with different colors and facial features (for example, dingos have a more dog-shaped face whereas coyotes closely resemble wolves apart from size).

You can also create domestic dogs from this tutorial. Of course, larger breeds of dogs work best when translating this tutorial over to a dog. You can attempt to make smaller breeds by starting out with a smaller wire skeleton and making your shapes based on the look of a breed. Get creative, and try out a few options.

Try out as many ideas as you would like: the options are literally endless!

Chapter 3:

Al-Pac-a My Wool

Alpacas and llamas. What really is the difference between these two animals? Is there even an important enough distinction between these two animals?

Although these two animals closely resemble each other, there are differences between them. Let us review a few to give you a good idea before jumping into the project. Both animals are native to South America and their coats can be harvested for wool/fleece. One stark difference between the two animals is that alpacas are significantly smaller than llamas. Also, llamas are bred and raised to be working animals whereas alpacas are bred specifically for their fleece. A common misconception about llamas and alpacas is that they often spit at humans. It seems as if the spitting is the only fact that people know about these two animals. In reality, both of these animals are unlikely to spit at humans. Spitting is a defense mechanism usually reserved for others of their own kind. Do they still occasionally spit at humans? Sure: it really is not that great. Camels have a similar response and it is just their way of saying that they are uncomfortable in whatever situation they are currently in. You cannot really get mad at them for communicating in the only way they know how, can you? I guess it all depends on whether or not you have just been spit on.

Alpacas are very intelligent animals and are extremely cute which makes them a perfect candidate to turn into a felted figure. They live in herds and are very playful and social. I think that is one thing that makes people love alpacas so much. I mean, have you ever seen a video of alpacas hopping around? Try not to look up videos unless you are prepared for a cuteness overload.

In this chapter, we will be creating a lovely little alpaca together. This project is great for intermediate felties because you can experiment with different colors and types of wool for this project.

Want to elevate your alpaca figurine to the next level? Consider using actual alpaca fleece! As I am sure you know by now, sheep's wool tends to be slightly coarse, especially compared to alpaca fleece. When you try out alpaca fleece for the first time, you will be stunned by how luxurious it is. Also, it is hypoallergenic which makes it a perfect alternative for people who are sensitive to natural sheep's wool. Plus, everyone that sees your little figure will be so impressed that you used real alpaca fur.

What is also exciting about this alpaca project is that it is great for trying out new and natural colors. Alpacas come in a variety of browns and whites, and most animals tend to be one solid color. This means that you never have to worry about trying to blend different body colors in this project. In the instructions below, the wool required for this project is listed as "natural color," so the choice is yours. Will you make a brown, tan, or white alpaca? Here in this photo, this little alpaca is a lovely tan color.

If you are not super familiar with the look of an alpaca, take some time to observe this picture below. Notice how the ears are rather pointed and sit higher up on the head than other animals. Also pay attention to how the legs are shaped. The body is lush and full of fleece whereas the legs taper down the hooves. From the side, alpaca's necks are very curved in the front but more angular in the back where they meet the body. Their hind legs have a natural curve, much like dogs. The natural curve of the hind legs meets a round belly. Finally, and perhaps most importantly, alpaca's tails sit close to the body and flop over in one glorious clump of fleece. If you are unsure of shapes, do a few more image searches to see different angles.

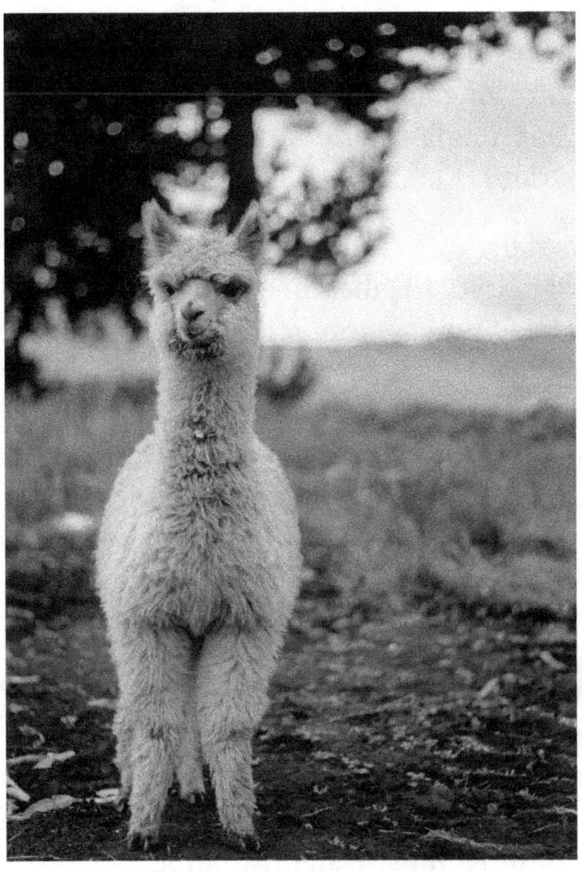

Alpaca Instructions

Materials

- Felting needles

- Felting pad

- Natural color (of your choice) and black roving

- Multi-needle holder

Steps

1. First, take out a large amount of natural color felt.

2. Divide it into three small strands (for the ears, nose, and tail), four long, slightly bigger, low density strands (for legs), one medium size strand (for the head), and one huge strand (for the body).

Pro-tip: When dividing and setting aside these pieces, it might be extremely helpful to label them. An easy way to do this is to find some sticky notes: write a quick note about which body part goes with which sticky note. With moving parts like this, it is extremely helpful to I.D. them at this stage of the game versus struggling to remember them when you are in the middle of the project. Do not worry if you have to set them aside with a sticky note; it is really hard to remember when you are trying to focus on the instructions!

3. Take one of the four long strands and give it a shape of an alpaca leg. These should be standard cylinders with curved bottoms for the feet. Remember from the photo that the legs taper down toward the hooves, especially with the fleece. Without the fleece, an alpaca's legs are rather skinny but still slightly curved.

4. Add toes to it: three should do.

5. Repeat above steps three more times to create three more legs of equal size and shape. Do not forget to mimic the natural shape of the hind legs. This is important to achieving a realistic creature versus a round body on stick legs.

Pro-tip: When making these individual pieces, remember to leave the one end loose for easy attachment later on.

6. Grab the small pieces of wool that you set aside for the nose, tail, and ears. For the ears, create rounded triangles. Create an indented center to give the ears a nice shape. The nose should closely resemble a rounded rectangle. If it is boxy, do not worry about it at this point: we will enhance its shape later on. Finally, the tail should be oval in shape on one end. Leave the other end loose to attach to the body. Be sure to hold up these pieces to your alpaca's body when you make it in the next step. Adjust your shapes when needed.

7. Now find the huge strand that you set aside.

8. Place it on the felting pad and give it the shape of an alpaca's belly. This should be a pretty standard rectangle at this stage. We will enhance the shape later on. Be sure to rotate it regularly to create an even shape.

9. Now find the medium strand that you set aside.

10. Give it the shape of an alpaca's head and neck. This shape will be one long cylinder. Do not curve the top for the head, we will add dimension to the face later with other pieces.

11. Attach the neck/head to the body.

12. Now take some more felt and loosen its strands. Tear apart sections until you have thin wool that you can see through.

13. Use these loose strands of thread to make all of those body parts puffier. Use multiple needles with the needle holder if you feel it is necessary. Remember that a needle holder or pen will help you move faster through this step, but a single needle will do the job just fine if that is all that you have available to you. If you are looking to make a smoother figure at this stage, be sure to use a thinner needle to smooth out the bumps and fill in any gaps or holes that might be lurking around. Make sure to cover the entire body and to add a nice round shape to the underbelly. The top of the alpaca's back should be relatively straight in comparison. If you want to get really realistic, encourage a neat angle where the neck meets the body.

14. Find the ears and nose and attach them to the head.

15. Take some more of the loose felt and use only one needle for this task. Add this loose felt around the nose and face to create a fluffier shape. Make sure to save room for the eyes. If you look at the photo of the alpaca again, notice that the fleece above the eyes is heavy and almost creates a hood. Whereas there is no extra fleece present around the nose. You can add extra fleece to the nose or muzzle area if you desire to create a really fluffy and even shape or you can leave it alone to add more dimension to your alpaca's face.

16. Find your legs and wrap loose wool around each one. Using just one needle again, felt the loose wool in place to keep the fluffiness going. Use a thin needle here again

to avoid having any large or rough bumps. Be sure that you do not cover the very end of the feet to ensure that you have a traditionally tapered look.

17. Carefully attach the legs to the body with loose wool. Make sure that there is not a division between the body and the legs. If there are any holes, fill them in with loose wool.

18. Attach the tail and fluff out the body once more.

19. At last, use black felt to add details like the eyes and mouth. The eyes should be simple and round while the mouth should be a typical fish hook shape.

Your alpaca is ready for packing!

Pro-tip:

Now that you know the difference between alpacas and llamas, consider changing this shape to resemble a working llama. Here, you can keep experimenting with mixed colors in a figure (llamas commonly have slight color differences in their coats versus solid alpacas).

In addition to this, consider experimenting with accessories. Because they are bred to be working animals, llamas typically have harnesses, blankets, and packs attached to them. Do some image research and never try to skimp on color! Also, be sure to adjust the shape slightly. Remember that alpacas are smaller than llamas.

Most of these projects in this intermediate guide are geared toward making realistic figures. However, this project is also a great opportunity for you to make an unusual figure. If you are feeling adventurous, try out some wacky colors—think blue, purple, or green!—to switch things up. If you do this, feel free to make its facial features more cartoonish. Add accessories like a hat or a bow. Also, try not to forget adding some blushed cheeks or eyelashes to reach peak cuteness!

30

Chapter 4:

Isabelle From Animal Crossing

Pop culture enthusiasts and gamers rejoice! Next up in our project list is Isabelle from the popular Animal Crossing: New Horizons game. This project is a great change of pace from the realistic animals that we have been creating so far. Isabelle will also test your needle felting skills because she has a distinct look and style. Try your best to follow the instructions to a T to create an authentic-style Isabelle.

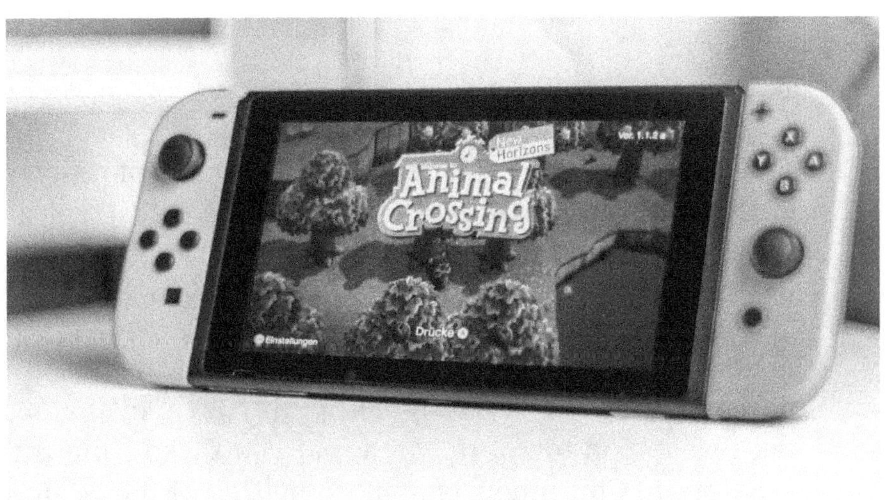

Isabelle Instructions

Materials

- Felting wool (oranges, pale yellow, red, white, green, and blue)

- Felting mat

- Felting needle

- Scissors

- Glue

- Jewelry cutter

- Head pins

- Gloss varnish

- Black polymer clay

Steps

1. We will start by making the head.

2. Use natural color felt (Isabelle is a light shade of yellow) and multiple needles to make a head. Begin with a typical sphere while leaving a section less felted as the whole head. This section needs to be slightly felted—it will become Isabelle's snout in the next step.

3. Start sculpting the face shape properly. Begin by poking in a v-shape on top of the area that you saved from the last section. Continuously poke along this v-shaped line that you have started to create dimension in the sphere.

When you are finished with this step, you should have a sphere and a protruding snout.

4. Then, make ears using orange felt. Isabelle's ears are triangular in shape and closely resemble floppy dog ears.

5. Isabelle's ears have two distinct ridges on them. You can create ridges by continuously poking at the same spot. Make sure to form a scalloped edge along the longer part of the ear and stop the ridges about an inch and a half from the bottom. When you are finished with this step, you should have two ears of equal size with three bumps (or scallops) along the bottom. At this point, you should check the ear size against the head size to make sure they fit. Isabelle's ears should fit from the top to the bottom of the head.

6. Now make a fish tail shape on your foam base in the pale yellow wool color. This piece will be used to create Isabelle's bangs, so make sure that the fish tail shape is wide enough to fit across the top of her head. Adjust accordingly.

7. Snip in the edges to create hair strands. Two snips with your sharp scissor about a half an inch should do the trick. This is to make her bangs appear textured when you attach it to Isabelle's forehead. Be sure to felt around the snips to secure the loose wool. You should not have to do too much felting here.

8. Find the two floppy ears that you just made and attach them to the head using loose felt.

9. Add your fishtail bangs. Use your needle to sculpt it properly. Here, you can create a neat parting of her hair

and felt the bangs to the head at the same time. Make sure it is secure.

10. Now create a bun using orange felt. Isabelle's bun sits straight up at the back of her head and resembles a slightly squashed mushroom. Add some dimension to her hair by mixing orange and yellow felt.

11. Find your sharp scissors and cut a small hole on the top of the head right behind where her hair part stops.

12. With the help of loose felt, attach the bun to that exact spot. Push the bun into the hole and fill in the hole with the loose felt.

13. Find a strip of red wool to make a thick hairband. This hairband will be created on the hair versus on your foam base. Add the red hairband to complete the bun. Make sure the red wool reaches all around the bun and touches but does not morph into Isabelle's bangs.

14. Find some thin white wool to use for Isabelle's mouth area. Remember to start with a little wool and gradually increase in layers as needed. Felt the white wool onto the protruding snout for mouth area detailing.

15. Now create some eyes and nose using polymer clay. Roll out a small piece of black clay. Cut this into small strips. Carefully press the strips into eye shapes. In this figure, Isabelle's eyes are closed and have a slight rainbow shape. Then, make a few noses by flattening small balls of black clay.

Pro-tip: Always make more clay pieces than you need, especially for such small pieces as these. This saves you time if they crack while baking or if you break them while assembling. Make lots because accidents do happen!

16. After giving the clay a proper shape, bake them as per package instructions. Once the pieces have hardened, you can pick the best shapes from your collection and save any extra pieces for other projects. Be sure to test the shapes on your Isabelle head now to make sure the proportions and shapes fit her head.

17. Now take golden head pins (typically used for making jewelry) and shorten them with the help of a jewelry cutter.

18. Now with the help of glue—any glue will do—attach the eyes and nose to the head of the pins. Make sure the glue dries completely.

19. Once the glue has dried completely, hold the pins upright in soft clay. Find your gloss varnish and glaze the tops of the eyes and nose. This varnish helps seal the clay and makes the facial features really pop!

20. Once the varnish has dried, poke holes in Isabelle's face where you want the eyes and nose to go. Add glue to the pin and insert them into the face of Isabella. Make sure to clean up any extra glue that might have leaked out before it dries.

21. Create and open the smiling mouth by using thin wisps of red wool. Again, start with very little and add as necessary. Leave a small rectangular shape at the top opening of the mouth for the look of a front tooth. By using thin wisps of red wool, you create a soft pink color much like the inside of a mouth. Go a step further by varying the red color from more vibrant around the curve to soft and pale pink in the middle where her tongue should be. You can even experiment here with 3-D shapes by indenting at the curve of the mouth.

Repeatedly poke the same area within the curve to help it take shape. Take some thin black wool and outline the shape of the mouth.

22. Set the head aside to start working on the body.

23. Sculpt the body using light green felt. Isabelle's body should resemble a triangular cylinder; just make sure that the top is not too pointy.

24. Add details and trimmings with darker green and white wool. In this project, Isabelle wears a green cardigan with two white buttons. You can achieve this look by creating a Y shape along the body. Place small rectangular pockets on either side of the Y. Then, add white wool to the curve of the Y for her undershirt. Take some thin red wool and create a bow on her white undershirt.

25. Create arms and legs. Start by using her pale yellow skin color to make curved arms. Add white wool to the top (think short sleeve) and create a puffed shirt sleeve. Create two plain yellow legs of equal length.

26. Attach arms to the body.

27. Now wrap the legs in blue felt and use needles to felt it in place. This blue wool is used to make a straight skirt for Isabelle. Poke until the blue wool is combined.

28. Attach the legs to the body with loose wool. Make it so that Isabelle appears to be sitting down.

29. Make a tail similar to a fox with yellow and white wool. The yellow wool should be at the thinner end that attaches to Isabelle's body and the white should be larger at the tip to create the illusion of it being fluffy.

30. Attach the tail to the area between her torso and skirt.

31. Felt all around to make sure the figure is smooth.

32. Finally, attach the head to the body with loose wool.

Pro-tip: Push downward when attaching the head to the body to help the pieces stick together well.

33. Now use different felt to add minor details and finishing touches like blushed cheeks for her smiling face!

Your Isabelle is ready to give out some camping fun and assignments!

Chapter 5:

Mighty Lion

I named this next project the mighty lion because lions truly are mighty. They may not be the largest land mammal—I am looking right at you, elephants!—but they sure know how to command respect. I mean, just look at that gaze! So much power and poise in one glance!

The lion used to have a much larger range across the globe, but now is mainly found only in sub-saharan Africa, with one extremely protected subspecies living in India. Like with other protected species of animals, conflicts with humans have disrupted the survival of these beautiful lions. Although there are a limited number of lions left in the wild, their legacy as the king of animals stays strong. How many stories can you name that feature a prominent lion character? Even in the past century, people have continued to revere and uplift the status of lions.

Think back to the first time that you ever saw a lion in person. For most people, this usually occurs at a zoo. For me, I will forever be in awe by how big lions are. Pictures rarely give a good enough idea about how large and powerful lions truly are. Are you ready to see if you can make a figure that will live up to the legacy of the king of all animals? We will find out!

Lions have some distinct characteristics. The most obvious of these is its mane. The mane, in its honey brown color, creates an almost halo effect around a lion's head. Remember that the mane stretches down the neck, onto the shoulder, and even between its front legs. Its body is a lovely sandy color to help it blend into its surroundings. Another distinction of the lion's look is the little tuft of fur on the very end of its tail. Be sure to include a nice array of browns to achieve the look of a lion.

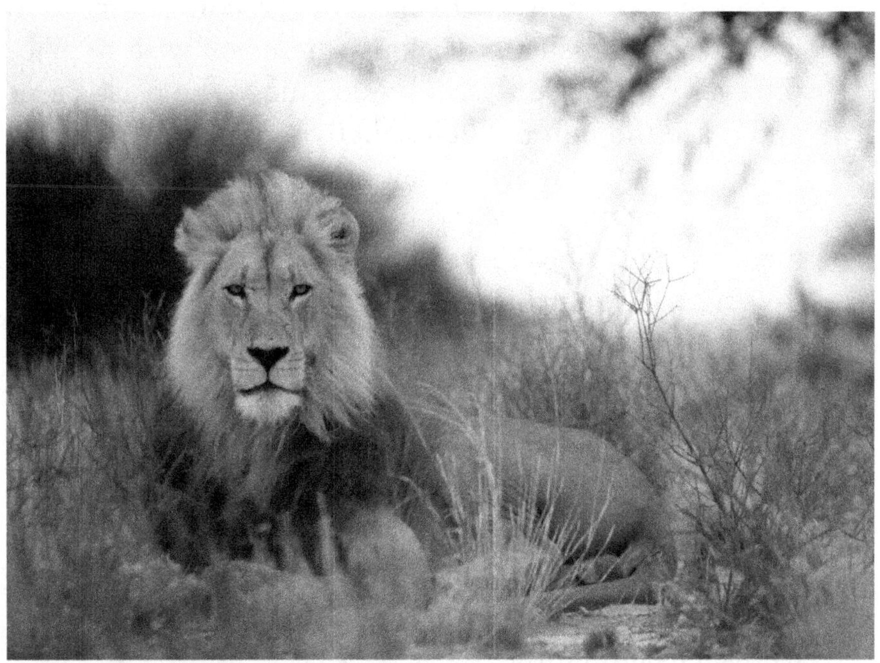

Lion Instructions

Materials

- Felting wool

- Felting needle

- Felting pad

- Artificial eyes

- Glue

Steps

1. Take a natural color wool and start creating the head. Add a rectangular shaped muzzle to the front of the lion's head.

2. When the sculpting of the head of the lion is done, add eyes by making small incisions where you wish to place the eyes with sharp scissors. Add glue to the plastic eyes and place them in the holes that you just created. I like to hold them in place for a few minutes to make sure that the glue begins to dry and hold the eyes in place. If you made the holes too big, you will have trouble at this stage. Be sure to wipe up any glue that might have leaked out before it dries.

3. After that, give highlights to the lion's face like the mouth and nose using black felt. Add some extra dimension to the face by lining around the eyes. Take a look at the picture above as an example. The lion almost looks like it has a great cat eyeliner—maybe that is where the popular cat eye look comes from. Who knew that lions were so fashion forward?

4. Make two round ears and attach them to the head of the lion. A lion's ears sit slightly off on the sides of the head. Try not to put them up too far and turn your lion into an aardvark.

5. Poke the inside of the ears repeatedly to create a slight curve in the ears.

6. Now take some brown felt and loosen it.

7. Add this loose brown felt to the head of the lion.

8. Add more details to it using some varying colors like light brown or a golden honey color.

9. Now add whiskers to the face of the lion using black felt. Be sure to make these very thin and small to mimic real whiskers. Consider adding small tufts of black felt to the inside of the ears to mimic ear hair.

10. After that, use natural color felt and sculpt the body of the lion.

11. Also sculpt four legs and one tail for the lion.

12. Take some loose brown felt and needle felt it on the lion's body, legs, and tail.

13. Now attach the body to the head of the lion with the help of some loose felt.

14. After that, add minor details to the body, using black felt to create paws on the legs.

15. Make a thin tail out of the main body color. Never forget to add that distinct tuft on the end of the tail!

16. Now attach those legs and the tail to the lion's body.

17. Take a huge amount of felt and loosen it.

18. Needle felt it to the figure from the edge of the neck of the lion to create the mane.

19. Use some more dark-shaded felt to add a second layer of mane to give it a more diverse look. Consider adding very

small strands of the mixed color like you did on the head to create a dynamic mane color.

20. Now take a very loose strand of felt.

21. Needle felt them on the lion's body at an angle in a backward direction: this will create a very nice hide of the lion.

22. Now, at last, use some colors to add more dynamic details to it.

Your lion is ready for stalking prey in the Serengeti.

Pro-tip:

The lion tends to be a much more advanced figure, which is perfect for elevating your skills! The mane gives you an opportunity to try out some loose wool skills. Consider creating a lioness to pair with your lion. All you have to do is adjust the size and skip over the mane: pretty simple! Now, you can start your very own pride.

Also consider going back to the wolf tutorial to make a spotted hyena. After you make an elephant later on in this book, you will be well on your way to making your very own food chair, but maybe try to not tell the elephant and the hyena!

Chapter 6:

Meek Winter Ermine

An ermine is an interesting little creature and very worthy to make it into your collection of needle felted animals. I mean, if they were good enough for Leonardo da Vinci, then they are good enough for you!

Ermines are native to Northern America, Northern Europe, and Northern Asia. A pretty wide span, right? Fun fact: in the 19th century, ermines were introduced to New Zealand to combat the rising rabbit population, but they ended up destroying the native bird population! Not so meek and little as they seem, are they?

In this project's instructions, we will be making a white ermine. In nature, ermine's coats change color based on their location. In the summer, an ermine has a sandy brown coat with a white belly. An ermine that lives farther north will shed its sandy brown fur to reveal a lovely all-white coat. Its entire body is white except for the very tip of its tail which is black. As you can imagine, this is to match its natural surroundings to help it survive the winter season.

Ermine fur was actually a luxury fur at one time which makes it pretty fitting to turn it into a felted figure! During its winter white, an ermine's coat is dense and silky. In the summer, its sandy brown top is coarser.

As I mentioned, we will be making an all-white ermine here. If you desire, you can make a sandy brown summer ermine. If you decide to do this, create the body parts as listed then add brown wool over the body parts. Check out this photo below to see the divide between the brown and the white sections of this little creature.

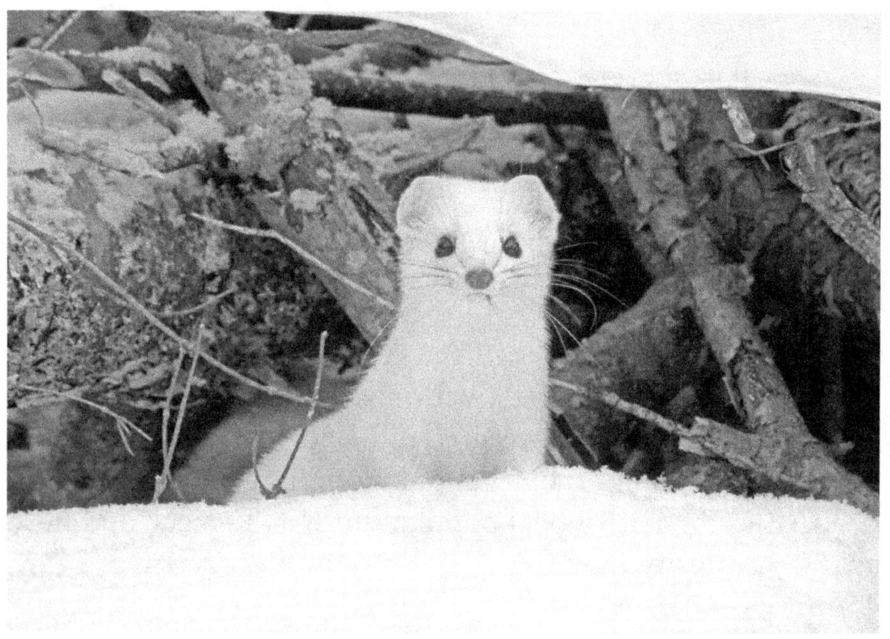

Ermine Instructions

Materials

- Felting needles sizes 36 (optional), 38, 40, & 42 (you can go higher if desired)

- Coarse wool roving

- White, black, brown, pink, and red merino wool (will vary depending on what you want to make)

- Natural horse/alpaca hair or clear fishing line for whiskers

- Glass eyes with wire loops

- Pipe cleaners

- Sharp scissors

- Super glue

- Needle and thread

Steps

1. First, make a wire skeleton/armature of your ermine. You can do this with either pipe cleaners or plain wire as we have done in other projects. Be sure to fold in any ends to make sure that the wire does not poke through the wool. Ouch!

2. Cover the head and body in roving wool. Wrap this tightly around the figure (do not do the full leg just yet). Add layers of wool to achieve your desired thickness. Felt the wool into place as you go to make sure that it firms up properly. Use a strong needle at first—36 or 38 will do— until you have a rough shape and your wool stays in place.

3. Move up to a 40 needle when you begin felting a denser body shape. Create denser areas with more layers as needed. Places like the shoulder and backside are where you should be doing this. Again, try not to add too much bulk to the bottom of the feet right now: just enough to

cover the wire. Do not move up to a higher needle because your figure will become too hard to work on if you do.

4. Now start adding some layers of Merino wool in your desired color. Merino wool is great because it is fine and soft. Use thin layers and a 42 needle to felt the wool in place. Be sure to add the Merino wool in the same direction that you added the roving wool to avoid a striped appearance. Ensure that the layers are thin so that they blend in with the roving wool well. Keep adding layers until the roving wool is completely covered. This will take some time and many layers.

5. Now create the tail. The tail has a cool loose look that will really elevate your figure; it also takes some time to make this step. Grab some strips of black merino wool and cut these strips into equal sections. If the sections are not equal, it will create a patched look. Fold the sections in half and felt them onto the coarse roving wool using a 42 needle. Keep felting the sides down and felt from multiple directions to make sure that the loose fur gets secured. You will know when you have completed this step when you can tug on the tail gently and the wool stays in place. Snip any unruly hairs to make sure that your tail is all one length and shape.

6. Sculpt the ears, leaving one end loose. Attach the ears to the head with the loose ends. Felt the ears to secure them. Make sure that the loose ends are felted so that they flow down the back of the neck in one direction.

7. Take your needle and felt repeatedly in the inside of the ears to create a slightly curved shape.

8. Add layers of Merino wool to the head to give it more shape. These layers will also help you create a denser head figure. Do not make the eye area too dense so that you can attach them in the next section. The snout of your ermine should be a nice rounded rectangle and protrude from the skull. The snout should also be firm up the center of the head to create a divot where the eyes will be. Add layers of wool to this center section to create this shape.

9. Add your eyes by cutting a slit and gluing the eyes in place. Make sure to wipe up any excess glue that might leak out before it dries.

10. Next, focus on the feet. Where you did not add much wool? Add a few thin layers or Merino wool to make sure that the pipe cleaner and roving is completely covered. Ermines have petite feet, so make sure that you are not adding too many bulky layers, just enough to cover.

11. Take your pink wool and make little paw pads and toes on the bottom of the feet. These are pretty simple circles and should be made using thin layers of pink wool. Start with very little and keep adding as needed.

12. Here, take your needle and thread to shape the toes. The thread should be the same color as your wool so that it does not stick out. Create four toes by using the thread to pull the wool in. This should look similar to a rounded scallop.

13. Add some very thin layers of pink wool to the inside of the ears.

14. Alternatively, you can also add some acrylic paint to add details to your ermine's face. Add pink to the ears instead

of wool. Add some grey tones around the eyes to add dimension and enhance the raised bridge of the nose. Create a nose with a reddish-brown color in the shape of an upside down triangle. Add any other details that you think you would like to create a truly dynamic little creature.

15. Finally, you can add whiskers to your little ermine with natural horse or alpaca hair or with fishing wire. Thread your needle with whatever material you are going to use and push it through the nose in equal distance on both sides. Add at least three whiskers for a realistic look and super glue them in place.

Your ermine is ready to do whatever ermines do.

Pro-tip:

Since ermines have been used in art and were once considered a luxury fur, consider elevating your plain ermine to a fancy ermine. Create a socialite figure, and give this little lad or lass some fun jewelry or even a bow tie and hat! These little accessory details are not only cute, but will also help you branch out and try new and difficult shapes. Also, consider making both a summer and winter ermine!

Chapter 14:

Funky Macaron Garlands

Whether you like to use garlands to decorate for a party, holiday, or other special occasion, you will absolutely love these whimsical macarons that you will thread into a funky garland. You might initially hang them up for a party, but this macaron garland might become a permanent staple in your home decor!

Materials Required

1. Felting Needle

2. Wool roving of different colours (One ounce of roving will make two one-inch macarons, so plan accordingly)

3. White roving yarn

4. Multi felting needle

5. Embroidery needle

6. Baker's Twine

7. Foam base

Steps to Follow

1. Cut a 48-inch long piece of colored wool roving.

2. Spread out the roving a bit to loosen the fibers. It is easier to work with flat roving than a wound up strand.

3. Take the stretched out roving and start to roll it into a tight ball shape.

4. Do not just roll it back and forth, because then the fibers will be very smooth and you will have to needle felt it for a longer period of time. Rolling the ball every which way will start to tangle the fibers before you take a felting needle to it. It does not matter if the ball is lumpy at this point because you will end up needle felting it into a slightly different shape.

5. Move the wool ball to the foam base so you can safely use the needle tool. You can use one or two needles at the same time, or even use a needle felting pen to prick the roving over and over again.

6. As you felt the wool ball, start to shape it into a thick disc that looks like a macaron.

7. While you are working, be sure to turn your work over and prick it with your felting needle from all sides.

8. Once you have a nice macaron shape, cut a 6" length of white roving yarn. Tie the yarn around the center of the macaron so it looks like the cookie's filling.

9. Make sure that the white yarn stays in place while you felt it onto the brightly colored macaron. You can felt this yarn just like you felted the wool into the macaron shape, but you will not have to work as hard. Just slightly felting the white yarn will adhere it to the macaron so it will stay in place.

10. When you have felted the white yarn all the way around the macaron, connect the ends of the white yarn so that it looks like a complete piece (and realistic filling!).

11. Cut the excess yarn off so that it will not hang from the finished product.

12. Repeat steps 1 through 11, using a variety of colors, until you have as many macarons as you would like to add to your garland. Once you make a couple of these sweet treats, you will be able to create them fairly quickly! This type of repetitive task is a great way to polish your needle felting skills.

13. Once you have all of your macarons ready, you can string them onto the garland.

14. Thread the baker's twine through the eye of the embroidery needle. You can actually use any thread to be the string of your garland, but Baker's Twine is sturdy and comes in cute candy colors!

15. Stitch the thread through the top layers of each macaron so the cookies will dangly slightly from the garland. If you want to thread the macarons through the middle, you can, but you might want to tie a knot before and after each macaron to keep it in position.

There is a lot of room for adaptation with this pattern! You can choose to make your macarons in pastel colors to look realistic, or you can use vibrant colors to make them brighten up your room. You can use two or three colors and make a repeating pattern on your garland, or you can use many different colors so that each individual macaron is unique.

Chapter 8:

Elegant Elephant

They spark joy and love for so many people, it is a shame that they are so big; I'm sure many people would love to have an elephant as a pet. After this tutorial, you no longer have to wish!

I am quite sure you have heard all of the facts about elephants. Elephants have an incredible memory, they have a lifespan almost the same as humans, and are so compassionate for such a large animal, it is no wonder people love them. With such distinct features like floppy ears, long tusks and trunks, and thick legs there is no other animal quite as unique as this lovable giant.

You are also probably familiar with the two distinct types of elephants: African and Asian. Although very similar, you can tell them apart by the size of their ears—African elephants have larger ears than their Asian counterparts. For this project, I will leave it up to you to decide which species of elephant you wish to make. When deciding which ear size to go for, remember that the shape of each elephant's ears closely resembles the continent on which they live. Pretty easy to remember!

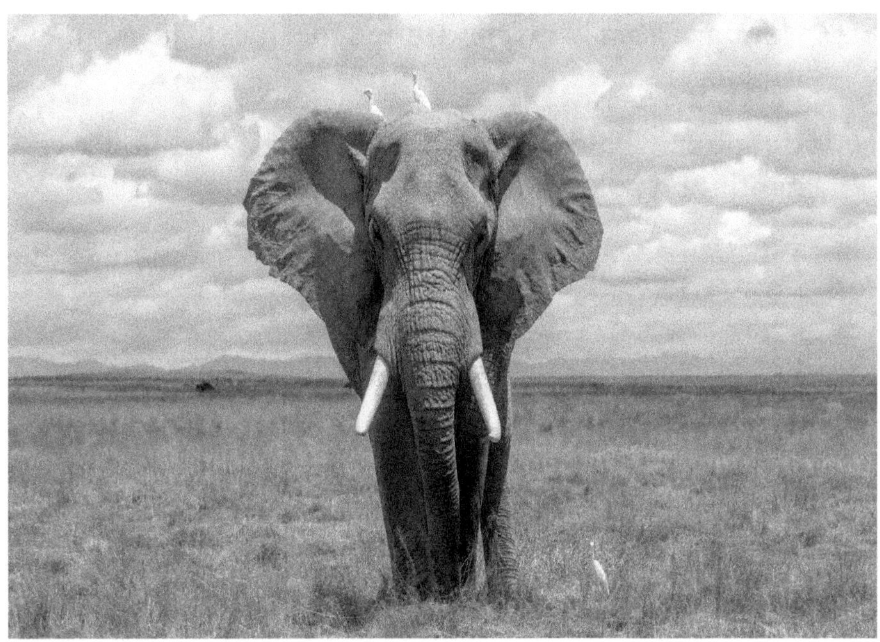

Elephant Instructions

Materials

- Felting wool (blue, black, and pink)

- Plastic eyes

- Felting needles

- Felting pad

- Metal wire

Steps

1. Start by taking a big chunk of blue wool.

2. Roll it out and start poking it to give it a circular shape.

3. Create one more ball but bigger than the previous one.

4. Now take a small metal wire and fold it in half. Wrap this wire together to strengthen it.

5. Wrap some blue felt around it to make a leg. Roll it very tightly and poke it to shape it firmly.

6. Take a really small amount of pink wool and make the base of the foot.

7. Repeat this process to create four total legs.

8. Now join your head to the body with the help of some loose wool.

9. Now join all four legs of the elephant.

10. Create the trunk of the elephant using the same technique you created the legs.

11. Use a tiny bit of pink wool to create the nostrils at the end of the trunk.

12. Now glue two eyes on the elephant.

13. After that, create the ears of the elephant. The size and shape of these ears depends on what species of elephant you are making.

14. Use pink wool to give finishing touches to the ears.

15. Attach them to the head of the elephant using some loose wool.

16. Now take some black wool and add highlights to the face.

17. Finally, glue a bow/flower to the head.

Your elephant is ready to eat some peanuts!

Pro-tip:

Which elephant did you choose to make? Now that you have made one, why not make the other? I mean, who would want just one elephant when they can have two!

Although elephants appear to be one solid color, their skin is very unique and wrinkly. It folds over in areas to trap water and creates areas of dark and light. Due to their natural surroundings, it is also common for elephants to have dust and mud on them to stay cool in their hot climates. Consider adding some small variations in color for your elephant's hide. This will help you create a more realistic and dynamic elephant!

Chapter 9:

Clever Fox

Very smart and playful, foxes have become known for their cunning thought processes and are often described in stories as intelligent tricksters.

Foxes exist on almost every continent, with the red fox being the most common of all the many subspecies. Foxes rarely pose a threat to human civilization, thus are seen as lovely and revered creatures. Some people even domesticate and keep foxes as pets. Due to their playful and loyal nature, they can be domesticated relatively easily. However, they are more common in nature versus households and do best this way.

For a large span of history within European countries, foxes were hunted for sport. This became a well-known sport among the higher classes. It was seen as a hard sport, given the cunning nature of foxes. The sport has declined significantly in modern times.

As mentioned above, there are many different variations of foxes throughout the world. In this tutorial we will be focusing on a common red fox. If you are interested, I encourage you to look up some different variations for future projects! You can never have too many different types of needle-felted foxes!

In this project, we will be making a standing fox. I love this figure because it looks very realistic but the standing form gives off a fun and almost cartoonish vibe. When I think of this project, I think of modern stop-motion animation. Check out the tips at the end of this tutorial to find some fun ideas about how to increase the animated style of this little creature.

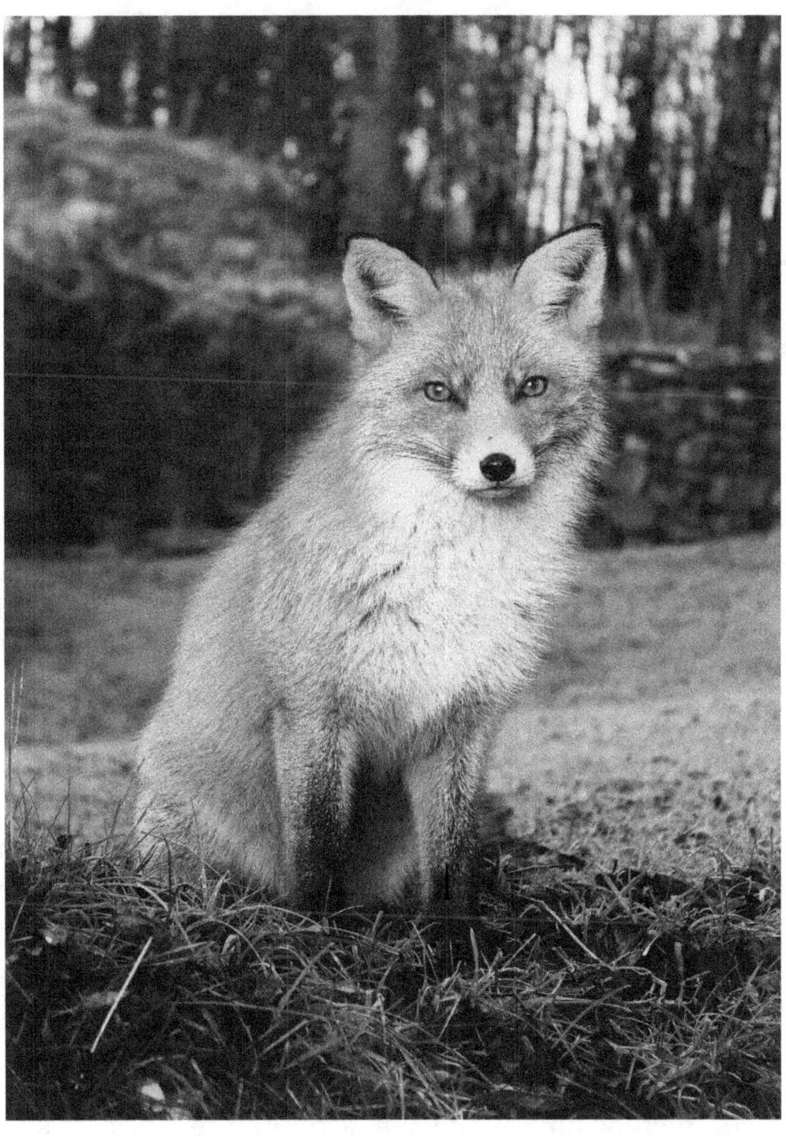

Fox Instructions

Materials

- Felting wool (white, orange, and black)

- Metal wires

- Felting needle

- Felting pad

- Plastic eyes and nose

- Sharp scissors

Steps

1. First, take white wool and felt a circular ball: this will form the head.

Pro-tip: For this project, it is important that you make sure to firm your ball (head) properly. This will help down the road when you add more color and shape to its head. Remember that foxes have very pointy features. This should take you a bit longer than you may be used to, but do not worry!

2. Now with the same white wool, needle felt an oval cylinder shape for the body. Again, take your time and make sure that this piece is very firm. Since we are not using a wire skeleton for the body, this wool has to stand up on its own. By taking extra time in these beginning steps, you are setting yourself up for success at the end.

3. Join them together with the help of some loose wool. Make sure that the loose wool seals the joining completely and wraps all around the neck. Also, by

layering loose wool around the joining, we are strengthening the figure and smoothing out the base. No lumpy foxes here!

4. Find your sharp scissors and cut to holes for the eyes. Place your plastic eyes into those holes but do not forget to add glue first! Clean up any glue that might have leaked out before it dries. Adding eyes now helps you to determine where various facial features will go.

5. Now grab some orange wool and make the nuzzle. Make sure to check the size against the face before firming it up too much.

6. Attach the muzzle between the eyes.

7. Take some loose orange wool and attach it to the face from the top of the muzzle to the forehead. Make a thicker layer to attach it onto the face. This should be slightly bulky against the small head shape. That is okay: remember that a fox's face is very fluffy!

8. Find some white wool in short strands and attach it to the face on both sides of the muzzle. This will start to shape the pointed fur that foxes are most known for. This will also help blend the muzzle shape into the head better.

9. Take a very thin strand of white wool and attach it to the very tip of the nuzzle—use a very thin needle here. Add thin strands as necessary but remember not to use too much right away.

10. Grab some orange wool and attach it to the area of the eyes. To do this, make sure you have a thin piece and cover the eyes. When you begin felting the wool, make sure not to hit the eye hiding below. Carefully work the

wool around the plastic eye to bring it back out. This section should cover below the eye to the white wool, around the sides of the eye, and well above.

11. Next, we are going to make eyebrows. Foxes are naturally very expressive, so this next step will help you achieve a good expression. Take a thin strip of wool and work it on your pad first to give it some shape. Try not to firm it up too much before you add it onto the head. It should still be loose and long. Use a thin needle here again.

12. Attach the eyebrow directly above the eye. There should be little to no gap between the eyebrow and the eyeball. Felt it into place and trim on the outer eye edge as necessary. The eyebrow should start and stop in a perfect arch right above the eye.

13. Make the bottom eyelid in the exact same technique.

14. Complete the eyebrow and eyelid on both sides. Make sure that they are even or else one eye might look swollen!

15. Grab your orange wool to cover the back of the head. Make sure to tear the wool short then attach it so that you do not have to deal with a piece that is too big for the head. Add layers if necessary.

16. Cover the entire back with orange wool in the same way. Make sure to leave the front belly white and ensure that there is a clean line between the orange and white wool.

17. If desired, take some extra orange wool and add volume to the cheeks. Make sure to stay just at the cheeks to create that pointed fox look. Start small and increase layers if needed. Be sure to blend the wool in smoothly. Do this on the other side as well to create an even fluff.

18. Now it is time to add some more dimension to the face. Add volume right below the bottom eyelid by layering with wool. Make sure you do not completely cover the eyeball. Add layers as necessary.

19. Now focus on the top of the eye. Add more volume to the top of the eyes just as you did to the bottom. This time, make sure that you are keeping within the arch of the eyebrow that you already established in an earlier step.

20. Find the white wool and tear it very short. Attach it to the white section on the cheek. This will help add volume just as you did with the orange wool and it will add that extra fluff that foxes have. Make sure to add the wool evenly to both sides.

Pro-tip: If you desire, you can take a very small, thin piece of white wool and attach it to the very bottom of the eyeballs. It should not be bulky and should be blended very well. This is not a necessary step but can add some fun dimension to the face.

21. Let us now move on to ears. Make a flat triangular shape in your dark color. Attach white wool to the inside of the triangle and mimic the same shape that you have already established. Make sure that there is a nice border between the dark color and the white wool. Make two and check the size in comparison to the head before you finish the shape.

22. Attach the ears to the top of the head. When attaching the ears, create a slightly concave shape to form a natural ear shape.

Pro-tip: To strengthen the attachment, take some orange wool and add it to the joining area along the back and front of the ears. This will also help blend the ears into the head nicely.

23. Create two small loose balls of white wool and attach them to the bottom of the muzzle. This is to form the mouth and lips of the fox. These balls should blend in evenly with the muzzle, giving just a slight scallop along the edge of the muzzle. Make sure they are even on both sides and make sure that there is a nice line separating them from each other.

24. Attach the nose. Here, I am going to use a plastic nose and attach it in the same way as the eyes. You can use polymer clay if you desire. If you have extra clay noses left over from Isabelle's project, you can use that here. Attach the clay in the same way with a head pin; do not forget to add glass varnish to make a nice shine!

25. Next, grab some white wool to make the lower jaw. This piece should be thick but not too thick that it is out of proportion with the rest of the muzzle. Start small and add as necessary. Do frequent checks with the figure to make sure that the proportions line up well. The lower jaw should fit in the area below the lips that we just created. It should rest just within those top lips and should not be bigger than that area. In a realistic figure, the top lips should look like they slightly cover the side of the lower jaw. Make sure there is a distinct line between the lower jaw and upper lips.

26. Add some dimension to the face by outlining the mouth. You can use thin strips of black wool for continuity but black acrylic paint also works to outline the shape of the mouth. Whichever method you choose, follow the

established lines of the mouth and make sure the lines are not too large. Add some black color to the top of the nose to blend the color between the black button nose and the orange muzzle. If you are using wool, use very thin strands to achieve this look. If you are using paint, blend the paint from the nose to out on the muzzle.

27. Onto the legs and hands.

28. For the legs, take your wire and twist it evenly to strengthen it. Grab some orange wool and wrap it tightly around the wire. Roll the wool around the wire until you achieve your desired thickness. Then, take your needle and poke it until it firms up around the wire. Find your black wool and add it to the bottom tip of the leg. Blend the black wool in well.

29. Make two legs of equal length and repeat the same process for the hands. Make sure that the hands are ever so slightly shorter than the legs.

30. Attach the legs to the side of the body. Add more layers of orange wool to strengthen the attachment and smooth out the surface just as you did for other attachments. By adding layers here, you are also helping form the natural shape of the hind legs which tends to be thicker on real animals.

31. Onto the tail.

32. The tail is created in a similar way that the legs are formed. Take a wire and wrap it evenly, firmly wrapping white wool around it. Add more layers to add the natural fluffy shape of the fox's tail. Then, felt the wool to firm it up. Find orange wool and add it to the tail on the top section where it will be attached to the body. This will

leave a white tip at the bottom. Make sure that the orange wool is much fluffier than the white wool to create that natural shape.

Pro-tip: Add thin layers of black wool to the orange section of the tail to create a dynamic color. This is not a necessary step but it helps to pull in the darker ears and the black of the facial features.

33. Join the tail at the backside of the body of the fox. Add layers of orange wool to strengthen the attachment and to add fluff to the backside of the fox. This will also help you blend the tail to the body and create a natural smooth shape. Make sure that you add layers of wool to all sides of the tail attachment. This will help make it even.

34. Take orange wool and add significant volume around the tail and legs on the body. This fox figure should have curvy hips and this area should be rounder than the top torso. Keep poking until the additional fur is smooth and firm.

35. Attach the arms in the same way as the legs by adding layers of wool to strengthen the attachment, blend the arms to the body, and smooth out the figure. Unlike the legs, you should be using thin layers of wool here because the arms should not have as much bulk as the legs. Make sure your layers cover all sides of the arm attachment. Keep layering with more thin wool as needed.

Your fox is ready to frolic through some fields!

Pro-tip:

Since we have created a unique, standing fox, this is a great opportunity to make it like a realistic cartoon character. You can do this by adding accessories to the fox. The best and easiest accessory is a lovely little scarf. Choose your favorite color or choose a color that you think the fox would like best and create a long scarf wrapping around the neck of the fox. If you are feeling adventurous, try out mittens or maybe even a lovely turtleneck sweater!

Alternatively, you can experiment with different colors/species of foxes. Think white for an arctic fox, or you can alter this design to make it more subdued and brown. You can either do this by following the above instructions exactly, but layer thin strands of black wool over the orange to create dimension within the color. Or you can start by using a more reddish-brown color (think like a rusty red or orange that closely resembles brown). Do some image searches to see what colors are available.

You can also create a fluffier fox by following the above instructions. When you come to the end of the project, take your needle and gently comb the wool in the natural direction that fur would grow, which is down. You can do this to all areas of the figure apart from the muzzle and the lower jaw. If you do this, be sure to trim some of the overhanging wool that you pulled away from the figure. You want your fox to be fluffy but neat.

Wrapping Things Up

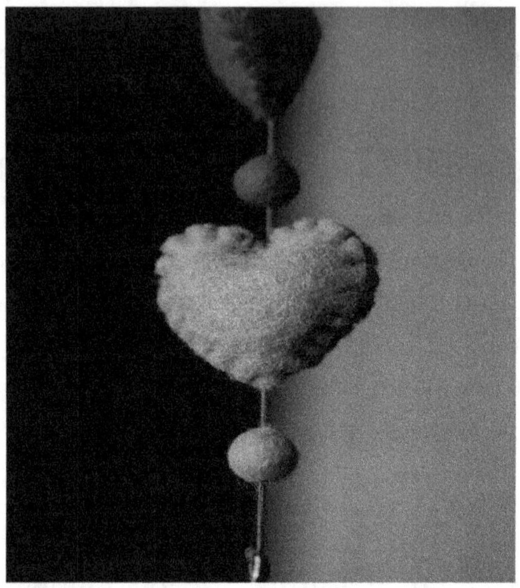

If you are reading this closing chapter, that means you just completed your intermediate guide to needle felting. Take a moment to pat yourself on the back! You did it! Now you have two full needle felting guides under your belt. May we say what a pro you have become?

Here we are, at the end of the intermediate guide to needle felting. Man, has it been a fun ride. I hope that it has been as fun for you as it has been for me. I also hope that you are loving all of the little creatures you just made.

I also hope that you are immensely proud of all the hard work that you put in to get to where you are right now. You would not be here if you never carved out specific time in your weeks to work on improving your needle felting skills.

I had such a fun time putting together the beginner and intermediate guides for you, and it fills my heart with so much joy that you took the time out of your busy schedule to sit down with me and learn the unique art of needle felting. While I may not know what led you here, I am so happy that you showed up and kept showing up. That shows dedication and makes you truly noble. Shall we start the knighting ceremony now?

Take a moment to pause and think about what created the spark that led you to want to learn how to needle felt. Was it a friend or family member? Did you see a perfectly adorable little needle felted creature online? Maybe you were gifted a needle felting kit by someone who thought you might like it. Take a moment to just consider what it was that brought you to pick up the art. If a person that you know got you interested in needle felting, maybe consider taking a few minutes to thank them for that. If they are a fellow feltie, invite them to grab coffee and talk about needle felting. Talk about what you most love about needle felting, talk about what you have most struggled with, and of course be sure to share photos with them of all the amazing little creatures that you have made. Chances are, you will probably find that you two share some of the same love and frustrations that are involved in this art form!

These guides were such a labor of love for me and were such a joy to put together. Please know that at every step of the way, I have been silently cheering you on as you flip from page to page. I hope that you felt a little bit of connection to me through my guides and that you feel like you almost got to know me a little bit, too. Writing this now, I feel like I am getting to know you, too! The art of needle felting is something that brings me great joy in my personal life. In creating these two little guides, I wanted to share that love and share what I have learned in my journey through learning needle felting with the hope that you can take something away from the advice I included in these guides. I also hope that both of these guides have fueled a creative fire and that you will keep stoking that fire as you make your way through new projects. As I am sure you know by now, the art of needle felting is extremely addictive. This is one addiction that you will not want to quit!

My main hope for you reading this guide is that you come away from this book more confident in your needle felting ability. Is there still more to learn? Sure! Like I said before, there is always something new to learn in this art form and that is what makes it so special.

Take a moment to celebrate how far you have come in just two short books. Look back on the very first shape that you created: a heart. Looking back on it now, you probably are shocked by how simple it is to make a heart. That shows you how much you have learned! If you have a few moments, go back and make a new heart. You can make it in the same color or material as your very first heart or something different: the choice is yours. When you finish making the new heart, set it next to your very first heart. Take a moment to notice any differences in your experience from the very beginning to now. Did you make the new heart faster? Is your new heart smoother? Does it have a more definable shape? Chances are, you will notice some difference. Revel in this difference. Revel in your improvement. You have come so far!

Together, we have started off with simple flat shapes and built up our structure skills. We learned how to make pin cushions, funky garlands (I still love that macaron garland so very much, and I hope you do, too!), and we began to take our first steps toward creating animal shapes. In this intermediate guide, we really stepped up our game. In this book, we used quite a few wire skeletons or armatures which are such a great way to start out a needle felting project. Wire skeletons not only help you create very detailed and varied shapes, they also allow you to create movable structures. Even after felting, the wire can be bent to give your figures new poses and shapes. How cool is that?

Beyond that, we learned how to use some brand new tools like the multi-needle holder and the Zullitool. Both tools are great to have within your armory and will be extremely useful as you continue on this needle felting journey.

In this intermediate guide, we also learned some very important tips, tricks, and advice. I hope you found some new tips and tricks to put into your needle felting tool bag. I also hope that those little nuggets of advice inspire you to seek out more information. With a growing community of needle felters out there, there is literally an endless amount of information available to you. I strongly encourage you to seek out like-minded individuals within the felting community. This could be online through blogs or videos or in person.

Maybe this journey has also inspired you to build your own community. Have you thought about starting your own blog to track your needle felting journey? At least think it over for a little bit. This could be a great way to meet new people and find more felties out there. Who knows, maybe you might even inspire a beginner who is struggling to find their groove. Think back to when you started out in the beginner's guide. What skills and techniques did you struggle with at first? Was there any information that you wished you knew before you jumped into your first project? Even think about when you made the switch from the beginner's guide to the intermediate guide.

There was a pretty big jump there. What were you most intimidated by? What techniques did you find that you had to practice over and over again? Take a moment to think about all of these things. Not only does it give you a pretty good idea about how much you have learned and how much hard work you went through to get here: these questions are not unique to just you. Chances are, there are lots of beginners just starting out and asking these same questions. You have the unique opportunity to become a leader and mentor to someone just starting out. Reach out: I am sure you will be awfully glad when you do!

If the online community does not really feel like your thing, consider creating your own in-person community. Start off with one or two friends or some colleagues. Find someone whose interest is sparked when you share your passion for needle felting and help them get started. Now that you know so much, you can be there for beginners to help them along their path. Encourage and uplift them, help them by answering their questions or maybe even supplying them with their very first needle. Needle felting is so much more fun when it is done with others. Find your posse. They will be there with you through *stick* and thin. Because people who felt together, stay together.

Now all that is left to do is to name all of your animals and animals variations. To me, this is such a fun little moment to really take ownership of your creations. Plus, when you are showing off your incredible needle felting skills to your adoring fans, you can introduce each little figure by name.

References

Anh, N. (2019). Elephant Walking. In *Unsplash.* https://unsplash.com/photos/QJbyG6O0ick

Binc Bonc. (2018a). Fox Needle Felting Tutorial [YouTube Video]. In *YouTube.* https://www.youtube.com/watch?v=-uc95YaHF50&feature=youtu.be

Binc Bonc. (2018b). Teddy Bear Needle Felting Tutorial [YouTube Video]. In *YouTube.* https://www.youtube.com/watch?v=lgZEcxdH4MI&feature=youtu.be

Constable, C. (2018, November 16). *Advanced Needle Felting Projects for Experienced Enthusiasts.* WonderfulDIY. https://wonderfuldiy.com/advanced-needle-felting-projects/

Dinata, Y. (2018). Black mouse. In *Unsplash.* https://unsplash.com/photos/k9NVUS7PS4A

How to Needle Felt. (n.d.). WikiHow. Retrieved November 8, 2020, from https://www.wikihow.com/Needle-Felt

Huaman, C. R. (2018). Alpaca standing on brown soil. In *Unsplash.* https://unsplash.com/photos/gdBqSojOV38

Kurfess, S. (2020). Blue nintendo switch game. In *Unsplash*. https://unsplash.com/photos/hzad7o11p5I

Lyashenko, O. (2019). Teddy Bear. In *Unsplash*. https://unsplash.com/photos/7XoKI25ufn0

McCutcheon, S. (2018). Free Love. In Unsplash. https://unsplash.com/photos/d55BPRk0dnk/info

Potgieter, A. (2020). Brown lion lying down. In *Unsplash*. https://unsplash.com/photos/GV2LxPJArgQ

Sandbakk, L. (2016). Brown Fox. In *Unsplash*. https://unsplash.com/photos/HQqIOc8oYro

St-Hilaline Poulin, M. (2019). White animal. In *Unsplash*. https://unsplash.com/photos/PSxIoipDUZ4

Tahoe. (2019). Grey and White Wolf. In *Unsplash*. https://unsplash.com/photos/Eaz0wqnV1VQ

Top 25 Needle Felting Tips and Tricks. (n.d.). Kawaii Felting. Retrieved November 8, 2020, from https://kawaiifelting.com/about/sample-page/my-top-25-needle-felting-tips-and-tricks/

73